ADVENT

to

Epiphany

From Text to Sermon

DR. A. D. BEACHAM, JR.

All Scripture quotations, unless otherwise noted, are from the King James Version of the Bible.

Advent To Epiphany: From Text To Sermon

Cover and Interior Page design by True Potential, Inc.

ISBN: (Paperback): 9781960024022

ISBN: (e-book): 9781960024039

LCCN: 2023932910

True Potential, Inc.

PO Box 904, Travelers Rest, SC 29690

www.truepotentialmedia.com

Produced and Printed in the United States of America.

Dr. Doug Beacham has done it again. His captivating pen has produced a gift for any pastor seeking to lead their flock through the first holy days that dot the Christian calendar. With the precision of a skilled surgeon he carefully and correctly exegetes the biblical texts. He then provides a clear path to preaching these truths in the most practical of ways.

These insightful perspectives from this recognized Pentecostal leader furnish a road map for ministers to lead their listeners *From Text to Sermon* through some of the most important days of human history. Thank you, Bishop Beacham for challenging the contemporary church to remain connected to our ancient and historical roots.

—Terry Tramel
Director of Global Outreach and Leadership Development
IPHC World Missions Ministries

Bishop Doug Beacham offers pastors a valuable resource for better understanding the importance of the church calendar as a tool of Christian discipleship. He helps readers see the importance of keeping sacred time in an increasingly secular world. Beacham shows how the biblical stories surrounding Advent and Epiphany offer narratives that ground believers in the unique message and ethos of the Gospel. Preachers looking for ways to lead congregations in the mysterious journey from Advent to Epiphany will be able to glean from Beacham's treasure trove of Biblical exposition.

—Cheryl Bridges Johns
Visiting Professor & Director of Global Pentecostal House of Study,
United Theological Seminary

I am convinced that the state of Christianity in any culture can be tied to the state of the pulpit. So much of Christianity is anemic because of shallow preaching built around creative hooks and catchy ideas but not firmly grounded in the Word. Bishop Beacham has offered us help in correcting this issue. If we will listen to him, our preaching will be richer; and when our preaching is richer, the pew will be healthier. Beacham's reasoned defense of preaching in the liturgical cycle offers a powerful strategy for disrupting the cadence of our world with the rhythms of God's grace.

—Ryan Jackson
Lead Pastor
The Capital Church, Raleigh, NC

In a time when more Pentecostals are opening themselves to liturgical spiritual formation, Dr. Doug Beacham offers them this edifying and enlightening text. He combines a Pentecostal hermeneutic with the Church's liturgical calendar; the result is a book that succeeds at its purpose – to offer and invite the readers to a distinct way for spiritual formation during Advent and leading to Epiphany. Using texts from the prophet Isaiah and multiple readings from the New Testament, Beacham helps readers focus on the meaning of Advent and Epiphany as well as challenges them to become better disciples. Relying on his expertise and experience as well as both ancient and contemporary texts, he guides the audience to a greater recognition of and appreciation for the merger of Pentecostalism with the liturgical calendar.

He challenges specifically Pentecostal preachers and pastors to utilize the liturgical season in their sermons. Rather than giving them an outline or an expository sermon, Beacham offers various possibilities for preaching the texts as they relate to Advent and Epiphany. The author assists this enterprise by moving the reader literally *From Text to Sermon*. The author permeates the "text' portion in every chapter with valuable historical and exegetical information to aid the reader in correct interpretation. If one requires more depth, the endnotes provide vital material and opportunities for further study.

Bishop Beacham's text is as practical as it is educational. If you are a Pentecostal pastor, this book will help you present the true message of the season before, during, and after Christmas. I recommend it highly.

—Ken L. Young
Professor of New Testament Language & Literature Chair
Department of Christian Studies,Southwestern Christian University

In *Advent to Epiphany: From Text to Sermon* Dr. A. D. Beacham, Jr. offers a guide for church leaders seeking to teach through the Christian seasons. He brings history and application. He presents practical examples of how the ancient stories can be alive and hopeful for today's hurting people.

By reading, learning, and applying Dr. Beacham's wisdom, today's church leaders can stand together with ministers through history.

—Chris Maxwell
Author, Campus Pastor and Spiritual Life Director
Emmanuel College

To my wife Susan. For fifty years you have made the Advent and Epiphany Seasons times of great joy for our family.
Your dedicated study of the Bible is a constant inspiration.
I learn much from your insights and discipline in all that you do.

CONTENTS

INTRODUCTION

This book is the first in a series designed to help pastors and their flocks better understand the rhythm and purpose of the Christian calendar. As Christians, we view time from a different perspective than the rest of the world. Oh yes, we use the same seconds, minutes, hours, dates, and days as those around us. But we view the meaning and purpose of history and the future by considering God's actions through the children of Abraham and through His only begotten Son, Jesus of Nazareth.

Thus, we hold that certain events in the Bible, though over two thousand years old, nonetheless provide the key to discerning the times in which we live. That's why we remember Christmas, Epiphany, Lent, Easter, Pentecost, and the like. We read the antecedents of these events in the Hebrew Scriptures and find their meaning through the lens of Jesus Christ and the Holy Spirit.[1] That's why we look seriously at the "timing" of "the old, old story" as we attempt to live out what I call an "ancient but present faith" in a society where biblical literacy is increasingly non-existent.

We begin with Advent, and this book will conclude with Epiphany. January 6. We start with Advent because historically and theologically, the Christian calendar begins with Advent, the four Sundays prior to Christmas Day.[2] We follow with some biblical texts that the historic church has determined should be remembered during the period known as the Twelve Days of Christmas.[3] Finally, we conclude with text analysis of the Epiphany, or revelation of who Jesus is for the Gentiles at the close of the Twelve Days of Christmas.[4]

While not the focus of this book, it should be noted that it is forty days from the beginning of Advent to Epiphany. It is also forty days that Lent is observed from Ash Wednesday to Palm Sunday and the beginning of Holy Week. The Bible often records the significance of forty days of spiritual preparation for God's people:

- Moses was on Mount Sinai to receive the Torah from God for forty days (Exodus 24:18)

- Jesus was tempted in the Wilderness for forty days (Matthew 4:2).

As we reflect on Advent (and Lent), we should have our hearts open to this season of transformation. Often over a forty-day period (about five and a half weeks), especially if we combine prayer, worship, and study of the Bible, the Holy Spirit can discipline us into significant new and different ways of thinking, acting, loving, and serving.

I can already hear some likely questions about this book and about using a liturgical calendar, such as:

- "I know about Christmas and Easter and maybe Pentecost. But why do I need to know more than that?"

- "I grew up in what felt like a dead and dry church tradition. I don't want to go through that again. So why are you doing this?"

- "We're not liturgical! We just let the Spirit move!"

- "I've got to feel the Spirit move me before I can preach."

- "I just open the Bible and see where the Lord leads me."

Feel free to add your question(s) and comments to those.

There was a time I had the same reactions. Like many of you, I grew up in church. In fact, I attended church for nine months before I was born! My Dad pastored a Pentecostal Holiness Church in South Norfolk, Virginia, and so, well, you get the point. One or more Sundays near December 25 were given to singing the few Christmas carols in our hymnal: "Silent Night," "O Little Town of Bethlehem," "Joy to the World," "O Come All Ye Faithful." Because we only sang these songs once or twice a year, we usually stumbled over the timing in the second, third, and fourth verses. On the Sunday nearest Christmas Day, there was always a simple play, often with children playing the parts of angels, shepherds, Joseph and

Mary (holding a doll), and three wise men. I was an adult before I learned that the wise men were not present when Jesus was born. Plus, seldom was there a service on Christmas Day unless it fell on Sunday. Even then, the service was usually abbreviated so families could spend time together on the holiday.

And yes, we sang Easter songs on Easter Sunday (but that's for another book).

As a younger person, I don't remember hearing the word advent unless it was used in relation to the Second Coming of Jesus Christ. A preacher would declare loudly, usually in a threatening tone, something like, "The Lord's advent is near." Later I learned that *advent* was from a Latin word, *adventus*, meaning "arrival."[5]

Things began to change after I completed junior college at Emmanuel College and my baccalaureate degree in history at the University of Georgia. Called into the ministry while at Emmanuel, I knew I should go to seminary and prepare to be a pastor with a Master of Divinity degree. In the early 1970s, there were few, if any, accredited Pentecostal seminaries, and many evangelical seminaries were not as interested in practicing Pentecostals. Besides, I already had some general understanding of the basics of popular evangelical/Pentecostal theology and wanted something to challenge me. So, I applied to Duke Divinity School (Methodist) and Union Theological Seminary (Presbyterian). Both were considered "liberal" by many in my denomination, but I still wanted to expand my understanding. Somewhat to my surprise, I was accepted.

Though my denominational theological family tree is rooted in Methodism, I ended up going to the Presbyterian seminary in Richmond, Virginia. The reasons were somewhat personal: the influence of a godly Presbyterian uncle and the presence of a strong Pentecostal Holiness church and pastor that wanted me on their staff. There was another very practical reason: the Presbyterians gave me a nice scholarship! For a Wesleyan Arminian who was exposed to John Calvin, that was the closest I came to believing in the old TULIP form of predestination.[6]

In Richmond, the rhythms of the historic church calendar merged from two directions. First was the seminary life, where the awareness of Advent, Epiphany, Lent, and the lengthy season of Pentecost were manifested in chapel services. The Seminary experience exposed me to the larger Christian world. Second was that the pastor of the Ray of Hope Pentecostal Holiness Church, the late Rev. Carl L. Campbell, had an interest in the church calendar. He taught me about these seasons. Part of the reason he did so was his own openness to the work of God beyond traditional Pentecostal and evangelical thinking. Large numbers of people from Lutheran, Episcopal, Methodist, and Catholic backgrounds who had experienced the gifts of the Holy Spirit had begun to attend the church. Pastor Campbell wisely sought ways to help them feel at home in a Pentecostal congregation. One way he did this was by using the liturgical calendar and changing the colors on the pulpit and communion table to reflect the church year. For five years, my life revolved around these two poles of a scholastic and pastoral environment where openness to God's historic work in His church was cherished and celebrated.

Seminary helped prepare me with knowledge concerning the Bible, biblical exegesis, theological thinking, and church history. The five years I served as Pastor Campbell's associate in Richmond helped prepare me for the practical, day-to-day life of pastoring. This was especially true in terms of preaching. From my first Sunday with him in January 1972 to when I left in March 1977, he allowed me to preach at least once each week in one of the three weekly preaching services.

In 1982 that experience proved invaluable as I assumed the pastorate of the Franklin Springs Pentecostal Holiness Church, the congregation that served the local community and Emmanuel College faculty and students in Franklin Springs, Georgia. From day one, there were three different preaching services weekly, and the responsibility of having "fresh bread" soon became a challenge. I learned different ways to approach that responsibility: times of expository preaching through a particular book of the Bible, preaching on various themes and topics, sensing the prompting of the Holy Spirit for His Word to the church on a given occasion.

What I had learned in Richmond gave me a framework for thinking through the church calendar and guiding the congregation into patterns of time that reflected the birth of Jesus, the meaning of His Incarnation, the reality of His manifestation to Jews and Gentiles, the call to serious discipleship in Lent, the remembrance of His life in Holy Week, the power of the Cross on Good Friday, the darkness of Holy Saturday, the joy of the resurrection on Easter Sunday, the empowering of the Holy Spirit at Pentecost for the mission of God's people in the world.

Perhaps many pastors do not relate to what I'm going to write. But there were times I wasn't sure what to preach, even after prayer and reading the Word. I discovered at those times that the use of the lectionary led me into Psalms, Old Testament readings, the Gospels, and the New Testament letters, arranged in such a way as to be complimentary to one another in sharing the message of the Word. I learned that if I took the time to carefully study, pray, and on occasions, talk with others, that the Bible, the Word of God, could and would speak on its own to God's people when I preached. I didn't have to be emotionally engaged in a certain style of preaching for the Holy Spirit to do the work through the Word. All I had to do was faithfully, and to the best of my ability, organize and present the message. Often, I finished a service thinking that I had done little to serve Jesus in that message, only to hear congregants tell me that God had spoken to them and they desperately needed what was said. In quiet moments afterward, I had this deep sense of the power of divine grace that was only dependent upon me faithfully exegeting and declaring the Word. It was not dependent on my emotive or communicative skills. That remains a very liberating lesson in much of my preaching today.

In the previous paragraph, I used the word *lectionary*. It is a source that contains portions of both the Old and New Testaments, usually organized around similar themes within those texts for a given Sunday. For instance, the lectionary readings for the First Sunday in Advent, November 27, 2022, were Isaiah 2:1-5, Psalm 122, Romans 13:8-14, and Matthew 24:29-44.[7]

As you will see in the main body of this book, I don't always follow the lectionary texts. Over the past years as IPHC General Superintendent, I have presented short Advent messages that are available at www.iphc.org/advent. These have tended to focus on certain characters and books of the Bible that related to the birth of Jesus.

That is the approach I'm going to follow as we look at Advent. In this book, I am going to use the prophet Isaiah as the Old Testament text and connect aspects of his message to how it was used and revealed in the Gospel narratives about the birth of Jesus.

The title of this book describes what this book is about. We will begin with a study of selected Old and New Testament texts that are appropriate for each of the seven Sundays from the first of Advent to the Sunday nearest Epiphany. We will examine the historical and literary context of the passages. We will look at key words and expressions within their context. We will look at how the church fathers, ancient and newer, have interpreted those texts. We will reflect on theological affirmations and on applications of the message of those texts as the Word of God to our lives and world.

Taking those insights from the text, we will move toward preaching/teaching ideas.

My goal is that the tools provided here, particularly the exegetical tools, will help you as you study, pray, and prepare to preach and teach the Word of God.

1

THE WHY OF ADVENT

CHRISTMAS, THE TWELVE DAYS OF CHRISTMAS, AND EPIPHANY

Simon Sinek's influential TED talk START WITH WHY reveals a key success factor for leaders: answering the fundamental questions of "Why." "Why" does our organization, project, book, or sermon exist, and "Why" are we doing what we are doing? Sinek called the process of answering this question, "The Golden Circle."[8]

"Why?" is the question I hope to answer as we think about the seasons of the church year. Let's start with answering the biggest "why," as in, "Why do we recognize any of these dates or seasons?" After all, even the Apostle Paul wrote to the Galatian believers, "You observe days and months and seasons and years. I am afraid for you, lest I have labored for you in vain" (4:11). Some commentators believe that Paul was addressing and criticizing tendencies to "Christianize" pagan festivals. On that premise, some have suggested that Christians should not recognize Christmas or Easter.[9]

I think a more balanced interpretation of the Galatian passage is that Paul was addressing a tendency among these Gentile converts to a) revert to syncretistic expressions that gave pagan rites power over the gospel; and/or b) perhaps these converts saw that adoption of Jewish special days gave them greater spiritual authority with their salvation experience.[10] Paul addressed the second tendency in relation to circumcision throughout this letter (2:3, 16, 20, 21, 3:10-14, 5:1-6, 6:12-15).

But before we jump to simplistic conclusions, we should remember that Paul kept the Jewish Sabbath, Passover, and Pentecost (Acts 13:14, 16:13, 17:2), and Paul alluded to Christ as our Passover in 1 Corinthians 5:7, Acts 20:16, 1 Corinthians 16:8. In Colossians 2:16 Paul advised that "no one judge you in food or in drink, or regarding a festival or a new moon or sabbaths, which are a shadow of things to come, but the substance is of Christ." The point is clear: it is the inordinate attribution of spirituality regarding the keeping of certain days and a failure to keep Jesus the Messiah as the central focus of those days that constitute the problem.[11]

This is the point made by Martin Luther in his *Lectures on Galatians*. When discussing Galatians 4, he wrote, "Whoever falls from the doctrine of justification is ignorant of God and is an idolater. Therefore it is all the same whether he then returns to the Law or to the worship of idols…. The reason is this: God does not want to be known except through Christ."[12]

It is this focus on the centrality of Jesus that answers the "why" of the importance of a Scriptural roadmap, which we can use to remind ourselves annually of the meaning of Jesus' birth, baptism, temptations, ministry of teaching/healing/miracles, death, resurrection, enthronement on high, and second advent. Some twenty years after the resurrection of Jesus, the Apostle Paul understood that the Old Testament functioned as "our examples" as Jesus was prefigured in the Exodus, the wilderness, and the fuller history of Israel (1 Corinthians 10:1-6).

There is another important answer to the question "Why?" It relates to how we discern time and God's work in human history. Philip H. Pfatteicher writes, "To the secular world, Sunday and the occasional holy day are seen as pauses in the routine of daily life." In the Church's Year, it is the daily business that is the enforced pause in the recital of the formative happenings that enlighten the ordinary days."[13]

In *A Secular Age*, Charles Taylor describes how Christian rituals served to unite the "spiritual work of monks and saints with those engaged in the routine, and often mundane, aspects of normal life. Taylor's book discusses the era when Christianity was the foundation of much of western culture prior to the Enlightenment and the dominion of modern secularism. James K.A. Smith, in his book on Taylor's work, wrote that "the social body in Christendom has a sense of time that allows even those daily engaged in domestic life that inhabit this tension between the pressures of now and the hopes of eternity. Rhythms and seasons create opportunities to live the tension."[14]

While Taylor's observation above reflected the ebb and flow of a dominant Christian calendar in the pre-Enlightenment era, it provided a framework that at least included an awareness, if even on the subconscious level, of the message of the Bible.[15]

Perhaps you have visited older churches in Europe or the United States where stain-glassed windows depict the story of the Bible. This was how church attendees, many of whom were illiterate, were able to "see," and therefore "hear," the stories from the Bible told by priests and pastors.

Smith's line from above, "rhythms and seasons create opportunities," is an important part of answering our secular world's "why" regarding the Christian calendar in the life of the people of God. Our secular world lives by the calendars of financial decisions, national holidays, and even regularly scheduled sporting events. We mark time by the human story and not by God's story. By looking afresh at God's revealed story, we discover the faint ticking of another clock, the slow turning of another calendar. It is a ticking that beats with the observation of Solomon near the end of his life, "[God] has put eternity in their hearts . . . " (Ecclesiastes 3:11 NKJV).

Advent, Epiphany, Lent, Easter, and Pentecost offer us the sound of eternity breaking into our noisy secular-driven age. It gives the people of God in our pews a "counter-calendar" that beckons forth eternity in our humanistic and agnostic age.

While you may be unfamiliar with the seasons discussed in this book, I hope you will find a template for thinking about the life of Jesus. An awareness of a different calendar helps us as we order our lives under the Lord of time. Our reflection on His life engages us in serious theological thought and in the dynamic work of the Holy Spirit, the Bible, and the Christian community, in making us disciples of Jesus in our generation.

What is Advent?

As noted in the Introduction, Advent occurs on the four Sundays prior to Christmas Day, December 25. Depending on the year, the first Sunday of Advent will occur on the final Sunday of November or the first Sunday of December.[16]

The word Advent is the Latin *adventus, to come to*. In turn, it was the Latin Vulgate translation of the Greek *Parousia*. This is plainly seen in 1 Thessalonians 4:15: "For this we say to you by the word of the Lord, that we who are alive and remain until the *coming* of the Lord will by no means precede those who are asleep" (NKJV). The italicized *coming* is the Latin *adventus* and the Greek *Parousia*. The Greek term is used twenty-two times in the New Testament, eighteen of which refer specifically to the Second Coming of Christ.[17]

This is important for several reasons. First, *Parousia* is a technical term used in the Greek/Roman world describing the coming of the emperor to visit one of his provinces or cities. When the New Testament writers Matthew, Paul, James, Peter, and John used this word they had in mind the personal return of Jesus to the earth to finalize His Lordship over creation.[18]

Thus, in many ways, Advent serves to point to the future Second Advent of Jesus, the Messiah of Israel. This is seen in the Advent hymn, *Joy to the World*, written in 1719 by Isaac Watts. Based on Psalm 98, the hymn points to the full redemption of the whole creation that was initiated in the faith of Abraham, made historical in the birth, death, and resurrection of Jesus, and will be consummated when Jesus returns. The words aptly capture the significance of Jesus' first and second coming:

> *Joy to the world! The Saviour reigns . . . While fields and floods, rocks, hills, and plains repeat the sounding joy.*
>
> *No more let sins and sorrows grow, nor thorns infest the ground; He comes to make His blessings flow far as the curse is found.*
>
> *He rules the world with truth and grace, and makes the nations prove the glories of His righteousness, and wonders of His love.*

This is an eschatological hymn pointing to Jesus' return and the Christian hope that the curse of sin finally will be removed. When we sing this song at Advent and Christmas, we are singing about the ultimate meaning of the death and resurrection of Jesus in preparing the way for the new creation (2 Corinthians 5:16-21; Isaiah 65:17-25; 66:22, 23; Revelation 21, 22).

Through two thousand years of church history, Christians have reflected on the meaning of the "comings," the "advents," of the Lord. The French monk Bernard of Clairvaux (1090-1153) wrote that Christ has three comings. The first was in the flesh in Bethlehem. The second is when Christ enters our hearts. The third is when Christ will return at the end of time.[19]

In the modern era, the four Sundays of Advent focus on "hope, faith, joy, and peace." Usually, there are four candles, one of which is lit each Sunday, and a fifth white candle in the center is the Christ candle, lit on Christmas Sunday.[20]

Advent is the beginning of the Christian year. While most of us give attention to New Year's Day in the West, the Chinese New Year in the East, or Rosh Hashanah (the Jewish New Year), the reality is that a Christian's year begins with the message of the First Advent, the first coming, of the Second Person of the Holy Trinity, the eternal Son of God, the only begotten of the Father, the Savior of the world. In the words of the Apostles and Nicene Creeds, Jesus was "conceived by the Holy Spirit, born of the Virgin Mary, God from God, Light from Light, true God from true God, begotten, not made, consubstantial with the Father; through him all things were made. For us men and for our salvation he came down from heaven, and by the Holy Spirit was incarnate of the Virgin Mary, and became man."

The development of Advent in the form we celebrate today has been a slow process. The Church of the first and second centuries apparently focused more on Easter, and perhaps Pentecost, than Advent. All four Gospels record the death and resurrection of Jesus. Only Matthew and Luke give any information about the circumstances of Jesus' conception and birth. It was the atonement, the meaning of Jesus' death on the Cross and His victory over death, that was the focus of the early Church. This is evidenced by the historical emphasis on the Eucharist and in the earliest statement of what constituted the heart of the gospel, "Christ died for our sins according to the Scriptures, and that He was buried, and that He rose again the third day according to the Scriptures" (Apostle Paul, 1 Corinthians 15:3, 4, probably 53 A.D.).

So, why December 25? Philip H. Pfatteicher attempts to trace the origins to Roman festivals that began on December 17 to honor Saturnus, their god of seed time. It was a time of relaxation, festivities, and even giving of gifts that developed into a seven-day celebration, thus concluding on December 25.[21] By the early second century, December 25 began to be identified with the birth of Jesus through the efforts of a Christian historian named Sextus Julius Africanus. Using the Julian calendar, he calculated Jesus' birth based on his chronology of the Bible.[22] Michael Judge cited another early Advent reference in the Spanish church council of Saragossa in 380 A.D. that required attendance at church services from December 17 to Epiphany. In the fifth century, Advent became a time of forty days of fasting beginning on November 11 to Christmas Eve, and by the ninth century, the dates were similarly established to the dates that Christians in the West use today.[23]

Judge also discussed another significant issue related to why church leaders moved toward establishing the celebration of Christ's birth around the old Roman pagan practices. It had to do with the second and third centuries' growth of the mystery cult of Mithras, the Iranian god of the sun and justice. Roman soldiers were attracted to this cult and brought it to Rome, where it became a religious rival to early Christianity. In Rome, the cult became an expression of loyalty to the emperor and was very popular among officers and regular soldiers. Mithras worshippers celebrated the god's birthday on December 25, a day they called "the birth of the unconquerable sun." The conversion of Constantine to Christianity in 312 A.D. led to the weakening of the cult within the Roman army, and Constantine's more favorable policy towards Christianity made it easier for church leaders to reinterpret pagan festivals with the message of Jesus of Nazareth.[24]

Recently these interpretations of alleged pagan roots to Christmas have been challenged. Citing an article by Andrew McGowan of Yale Divinity School, Kevin de Young argues from early church traditions that Jesus died on the same date that he was conceived. Assuming Jesus died during Passover during March, church fathers counted back to late December for His birth.[25]

In light of competing arguments related to the timing of December 25, we need to remember that the Gospel writers made no efforts to identify the date, other than it occurred when Caesar Augustus commanded a Roman Empire census or taxation, means that the exact date is of no theological consequence.[26] From Scripture, we know the following about Jesus's birth: 1) Jesus was born in Bethlehem, the city of David, located about five miles south of Jerusalem. Jesus' birthplace is significant as it fulfilled Scripture and connected Jesus to the family lineage of David; 2) the Apostle Paul viewed Jesus' birth as in "the fullness of time, God sent forth His Son, born of a woman, born under the law" (Galatians 4:4). The exact date was not as important as the facts that Jesus came from the presence of the Father, that Jesus was not a mythological figure but was truly born into humanity through a woman, that Jesus was born a Jew, and that Jesus was a member of the covenant family that traced its roots to Abraham, Moses, and David (especially to David as the fulfillment of 2 Samuel 7:12-17).

Today, most biblical texts associated with Advent focus on the following themes:

First Sunday of Advent: eschatology and the consummation of the plan of redemption for all creation. For instance, Isaiah 52:8-10 and Ezekiel 43:1-4. Both Isaiah 52 and Ezekiel 43 are prophetic words of encouragement and hope to the Jews in exile in Babylon following the destruction of Jerusalem in 586 B.C. Ezekiel, already in exile in the year 597, had seen in a vision the Spirit of God, the glory of God, leave Solomon's temple due to the sinfulness and rebellion of unrepentant Judea (Ezekiel 10, especially verse 18). In Ezekiel 43, the prophet sees the glory return to Jerusalem.

Second and Third Sundays of Advent: the role of John the Baptist as the forerunner of Jesus. Old Testament texts include Isaiah 26:1, 2; 35:2-5; 40:1-8; Habakkuk 2:3; Malachi 4:5, 6. The New Testament text cluster around Luke 1:5-25, 39-80; John 1:1-33; 3:22-36.

Fourth Sunday of Advent: the biblical texts related to Mary, Joseph, and the birth narratives of Matthew 1 and Luke 1, 2.

Many churches enter the Advent season with a special service of the "hanging of the greens." [27] Wreaths are placed on the church doors and windows, and often a Chrimson tree is set up in the church. The altar is prepared with the five Advent candles. They are usually arranged with four candles that are lit one by one through the four Sundays of Advent.[28] The fifth candle, a larger white candle, is the Christ candle which is lit on Christmas Eve or Christmas Day.

2

THE FIRST SUNDAY OF ADVENT

Isaiah 40:1-11

In this chapter, we will explore a cluster of Old and New Testament texts related to the mission of John the Baptist. Likely, you will not use all of these in preparing for the First Sunday of Advent; however, they will give you a framework for future messages for your congregation.

In this book, I will discuss passages from Isaiah for each of the four Sundays of Advent. Because of that, it is important that we begin with a general overview of Isaiah in its historical and literary context. The comments in this section will be important as you reflect on the specific texts for Advent.

The Historical Context of Isaiah

The prophet Isaiah received his prophecies during the latter reign of Judah's King Uzziah (called Azariah in 2 Kings 14:21) and the reigns of Jotham, Ahaz, and Hezekiah. This period is described in the historical books of 2 Kings 14:21 - 20:21 and 2 Chronicles 26:1 - 32:33. These historical sections give you a larger lens through which to view Isaiah's ministry. The time frame from the beginning of Uzziah's reign to the death of Hezekiah was approximately 90 years (783 – 687 B.C.).

The years covered in Isaiah 1-39 reflect several historical factors:

1. Isaiah's ministry began in the year that Uzziah died, about 740 B.C. (see Isaiah 6). But we should remember the prophet was alive during the latter part of Uzziah's reign when the king was isolated due to

leprosy. Uzziah's son Jotham served as co-regent with his father during the leprosy years.[29]

2. Isaiah was a "court prophet"; he had access to the king. Like any position of influence, a court prophet could be a genuine voice of God "speaking truth to power" or could be a sycophant for his/her own gain. Isaiah was a genuine prophet of God positioned to inform leadership of the ways of the Lord even if leadership refused to accept it. We will see this dynamic when we study Isaiah 7.[30]

3. By the time of Isaiah, prophetic ministry was well established in Israel's history. The prophet Samuel was instrumental in the formation of the first dynasty of Saul and later in the second dynasty of David. In David's time, the role of court prophet was held by Nathan, who also served during part of the time of Solomon. The prophets Micah, Hosea, and Amos, were contemporaries of Isaiah, with Hosea and Amos directly addressing the spiritual rebellion of the Northern Kingdom. It is likely that Micah and Isaiah knew one another personally. They may also have known Hosea and Amos and their messages.

4. The Northern Kingdom rebelled against Jerusalem in 922 following the death of Solomon. The cause of this rebellion is described in 1 Kings 11:26 - 12:33. God raised up Elisha and Elijah as prophets who gave divine utterances as well as miracles in their witness to the Lord. These men prophesied in the ninth century (800s B.C.) and were forerunners of the written prophets in the eighth century (700s).

5. It is important to remember that when Old Testament prophets gave a word of the Lord to a king or situation, they were knowledgeable of the Torah, the written record of Moses found in Genesis through Deuteronomy. They were keenly aware of the Ten Commandments and the blessings and curses of Deuteronomy 27, 28. They were also aware of the political and economic forces shaping their environment. They were aware of history, and cognizant of God's perspective on such matters based upon the Torah. Thus, as prophets of God, they were keenly aware of their contemporary events/history and of what the Lord's purposes were for the sons and daughters of Abraham.

6. The Assyrian Empire is the primary political/military power during Isaiah's lifetime and is the international backdrop for Isaiah 1-39. This

empire rose to great prominence in the reign of Tiglath-pileser III (745-727) and exerted its military and cultural influence almost everywhere east of the Mediterranean Sea.

7. The Northern Kingdom of ten tribes, usually called Israel, Ephraim, or Samaria, was conquered in 722 by the Assyrian King Sargon II. These tribes were scattered and lost their identity through the Assyrian policy of dispersing conquered peoples among other conquered peoples, diluting the ethnic, social, and religious connections that shaped permanent culture. In return, the Assyrians populated the territory of the Northern Kingdom with non-Israelite peoples. We will see this at work in Isaiah 9.

8. During the reign of Hezekiah, especially towards the end of his reign, Isaiah recognized the emergence of a new empire, the Babylonian Empire. The Babylonians would conquer Assyria and lead to the defeat of Judah (the Southern Kingdom of two tribes, Judah and Benjamin) and the destruction of Solomon's Temple (Assyria was conquered 609 B.C., and Jerusalem was conquered in 586 B.C.; see Isaiah 39).

Tradition holds that Isaiah was martyred during the reign of Manasseh (687-642 B.C.). Hebrews 11:37 may be a reference to the way Isaiah died.

The Literary Framework of the book of Isaiah

The prophecy of Isaiah is composed of prose and poetry. Isaiah 1-39 is primarily poetry with prose where the prophet is describing specific episodes, and poetry comprises most of Isaiah 40-66. It has often been observed that the book falls into three sections: Isaiah 1-39 reflects events during the lifetime of Isaiah; Isaiah 40-55 indicate the period around 540 when the Persian king Cyrus granted the Jews in Babylon freedom to return to Jerusalem; and Isaiah 56-66 reflects the period about 520 after the return has occurred and the restoration in Judea is in progress.[31]

The literary structure leads to questions concerning the authorship of the entire book. It should be noted that copies of Isaiah 1-66 have been a unity since at least 200 B.C. It was a unity in the time of Jesus as evidenced by His quotation of Isaiah 61:1, 2 in Luke 4:18, 19. It was also a unity in the famous Dead Sea Scroll of Isaiah.

I suggest the following approach to the literary issues related to Isaiah. First, there is little doubt that Isaiah 1-39 was composed by the prophet himself. Second, Isaiah's awareness of Babylon in Isaiah 13:1-22, 14:3-23, 21:9, as well as Isaiah 39, reveal that the prophet was not unaware that "the Holy One of Israel" was sovereign Lord over the nations and that nations rise and fall at His command.[32] It is not unreasonable to assume a genuine "prophetic" vision about 700 B.C. enabling Isaiah to see the rise of Babylon as an Empire threatening Judah a hundred years later.

As mentioned above, the genuine Old Testament prophets were students of history and Deuteronomy. Isaiah's analysis of Judah's sins, plus his knowledge of the incorrigible corruption of Manasseh (687-642), gave the prophet insight into a time of judgment upon Judah just as judgment had come upon the Northern Kingdom in 722. The difference was that Isaiah recognized the certainty of the covenant God had made with Abraham and that Judah, the remnant, would not be totally destroyed as had occurred with the Northern Kingdom. Thus, the message of Isaiah 40-66 provided a prophetic hope to the exiled Judeans, and Isaiah was able to articulate that hope with great clarity and application. Thus, without doing violence to the text of Isaiah, we can view the book as a whole and still affirm the historical context of Isaiah 40-55 and 56-66.[33]

FROM TEXT …

Isaiah 40:1-11 - The historical situation of Isaiah 40 has been referenced in the previous section. That background is critical for understanding the whole book of this prophecy and for understanding much of the Old Testament and the background of the New Testament. Isaiah was probably in the latter years of his life when the content of Isaiah 40-66 was revealed to him. Likely the corruption of Manasseh was the historical event through which the Holy Spirit gave Isaiah the prophetic vision of the impending Babylonian conquest. The prophet discerned the magnitude of the destruction as an instrument of divine judgment. Thus, chapters 40-66 became a vision of comfort and hope to a people devastated by their own sinfulness and rebellion against "the Holy One of Israel."

Between Isaiah 39 and 40 is a period of approximately 115-162 years. Remember that the Lord extended Hezekiah's life 15 years, making Isaiah 38 about 702/701. While the exact date of the Babylonian visit in Isaiah 39 cannot be established, it likely occurred within a year or two of Hezekiah's recovery. It was 115 years from Hezekiah's recovery to the destruction of Jerusalem in 587 and 162 years from Hezekiah's recovery to the end of the exile, about 540/538.

Brueggemann called this time gap "a pause – a long pause."[34] Details of what occurred in that "long pause" are expressed in Ezekiel, Daniel, parts of Jeremiah and Lamentations, and Psalm 137.

With this background in mind, let's review the key portions of Isaiah 40. First, notice that the entire prophecy related to the exile begins with a double plural imperative *comfort*. It is a message to the remnant who have survived in Babylon. Remember, they have been there 70 years, and Jeremiah instructed the captives to make a new life there (Jeremiah 29:5, see also Jeremiah 25, 30, 31). But the prophetic word through Jeremiah (and Ezekiel) always contained the divine promise of restoration back to the land promised to Abraham.

The word *comfort* is the Hebrew *nacham* (נחם) and is used 17 times in 13 verses, including Isaiah 12:1; 22:4; 40:1; 49:13; 51:3, 12, 19; 52:9; 61:2; and 66:13. The double use is a Hebraic way of emphasis. The word conveys compassion and consolation. In this sense, the comfort means that Judah's "warfare is ended, that her iniquity is pardoned; for she has received from the Lord's hand double for all her sins" (40:2). This is not the comfort a pastor gives a grieving person over the loss of a loved one. This is the comfort that comes from knowing that judgment has come to an end. There is a price to be paid for sin. Yes, Jesus has paid that price on the Cross for our forgiveness, but all of us know there is a price in our own spirit and among our fellows. The analogy is one of a restoration process whereby Judah, in captivity, has faced her iniquity and returned to the mercies of God.

The *warfare* of 40:2 has been Judah's obstinate refusal to *amend* her ways in light of God's revealed law (Jeremiah 7:3). That rebellious spirit was in-grained deep in Judah's people. This is revealed in the word *iniquity* (*avon*, עון). It denotes perversity, a twisting of the inner self individually and cor-porately. It is the reality of our fallen nature as human beings. The only way to remove this corruption of the personal and national self is by the sanctifying blood of Jesus and the presence and power of the Word of God.

The use of *double* in verse 2 indicates that Judah's specific sinful acts against the divine law (*sins*) are forgiven, and her propensity for sinful acts (*iniquity*) have been *pardoned* (*ratsah*, רצה). To be pardoned means that God is pleased with something; He has been satisfied with what has occurred in Judah's heart through these 70 years. God evidenced a change in their collective spirit. That God deals with our double sinful condition of actual transgressions, as well as our fallen nature, is at the heart of the atonement in justification and sanctification. The hymn *Rock of Ages* by Augustus Toplady (1776) captures this reality: "Rock of Ages, cleft for me, let me hide myself in thee; let the water and the blood, from thy wounded side which flowed, be of sin the double cure; save from wrath and make me pure."

Toplady's hymn leads us to how God dealt with Judah's sin. God did it through His Suffering Servant, as described in Isaiah 53. In this sense, Judah herself is the suffering servant, though prophetically, the Suffering Servant of Isaiah 53 is Jesus, the Messiah of Israel. Throughout Isaiah 53, the issue of *iniquity* is forefront (vv. 5, 6, 11) and the price paid by the Servant *pleased the Lord* (v. 10). It was God, through His Son Jesus, who paid the total price for our sins. It was God's holiness that had to be satisfied, a holiness that manifested itself in the reality of the fullness of love. God's holy love cannot be tolerant of sin. God's holy love often patiently withholds judgment and divine wrath for the sake of His holy name in order that the sinner may repent and enter the fullness of our destiny. But it is God who makes the provision for our forgiveness. Thus, it is *by grace we are saved* (Ephesians 2:5), and by grace, we are sanctified (Hebrews 2:10-13). This is why Isaiah 40:2 makes it clear that the pardon and the comfort are *from the Lord's hand*. Only God can deliver from the destruction of sin and restore Judah and us to His glory.

This is the framework for the key portions of Isaiah 40 that relate to the first Sunday of Advent. This price of restoration had to be paid in full for the future to be unfolded. God's gracious act of justification and sanctification is necessary for the preparation of the future God has in store for *My people* (v. 1).

I mentioned the double imperative plural of *comfort* in verse 1. There is a second plural imperative that begins verse 2 in the word *speak*. The content of this imperative is interesting. The NKJV reads to *speak comfort to Jerusalem*. Without question that is the intent, based on v. 1. But an interesting change in language occurred with the Hebrew, usually translated *comfort* in verse 2. The Hebrew text and the Septuagint (LXX) read literally *speak upon or into the heart of Jerusalem*. The word in Hebrew is *leb* (לב) and *kardia* (καρδια) in the LXX and usually means *heart*.

There is a double reason why Isaiah used this word in 40:2: 1) the prophet wants to emphasize the depth of the comfort announced in 40:1 as going to the "heart of the matter" and bringing genuine *comfort* to the exiles; 2) the *heart* is the seat of the will, emotions, intentions and is the source of where the perversity of iniquity finds its origin. As Jeremiah 17:9 clearly states, "the heart (same word as in Isaiah 40:2) is deceitful above all things." The message of the Lord to the exiles is that God is effectively dealing with their heart condition and the perversity that has alienated them from His presence and blessings.

Isaiah 40:3 begins with a singular voice crying in the wilderness that the deliverance is nigh and preparation must begin. As in the previous imperative verbs of *comfort* and *speak*, the announcement of *prepare* is plural. But interestingly, the focus of the preparation is not only on the exiles preparing themselves, but the preparation is for *the way of the Lord.* Just like Psalm 118:23, the exile is the Lord's doing. It is the Lord's possession that will leave Babylon and return to Jerusalem (remember the *My people* of 40:1). The references to the highway, valley, and mountain in verses 3 and 4 are metaphors indicating that nothing will interfere with this sovereign act of grace initiated from the heart of God.

Isaiah 40:5 places a dual emphasis on the *glory of the Lord* and *the mouth of the Lord has spoken*. God's glory is more than radiance or something around the divine throne that glows. God's glory is that what He wills, what He speaks, is accomplished. God's glory is revealed to humanity through His righteous acts that are visible in human history. When God speaks, His will occurs and comes into being. This is the entire point of Genesis 1 and God's speaking creation into existence. This is the point of *the Word made flesh* in John 1:1-14 and the glory of God being revealed in the suffering, death, and resurrection of the eternal Word, Jesus. That *all flesh shall see it* means that God's revelation is not hidden from humanity. It is only our willful disobedience and pride that keep us from seeing what God has made plain (see the Apostle Paul's arguments in Romans 1, 2 and 1 Corinthians 1:18 - 2:16).

The certainty of God's word is reinforced in Isaiah 40:6-8. It seemed impossible to the exiles' natural understanding that they could be restored. But the message of the one crying out is that *the word of our God stands forever.*

Isaiah 40:9-11 introduces us to the gospel. In Isaiah, it's the language of *good tidings*. In Hebrew, it's *basar* (בשׂר), and the LXX uses the participle form of *euangelizo* (ευαγγελιζω). Brueggemann captures the power of the *gospel* in these phrases, "*The news is that Yahweh has won, Babylon has lost, Judah is free.*"[35]

New Testament Use of Isaiah 40

The four canonical Gospel writers include Isaiah 40:3 in connection to the ministry of John the Baptist, the cousin of Jesus, as the forerunner who is preparing *the way of the Lord.*

1. Matthew 3:3 identified John the Baptist as the one that Isaiah foretold. John preached in the wilderness of Judea. There is some speculation that he was influenced by the community at Qumran. While direct connections are speculative, there is no doubt that the Jews in Qumran saw themselves as the fulfillment of Isaiah's prophecy.[36] John's message of preparing the way of the Lord was a message of repentance. While Isaiah 40 focused primarily on restoration, some 500 years after the exile John was anointed to call Israel back to genuine worship of God and be prepared for God to be among them personally through the Messiah. Another characteristic of John's preaching is to announce that the Messiah will baptize people with the Holy Spirit and fire (3:11).

2. Mark 1:2, 3 added Malachi 3:1, the last book of the Old Testament, to the Isaiah 40 citation. John the Baptist is not only the voice crying in the wilderness; he is the Lord's messenger who will prepare the Lord's way. Again, the focus is on repentance and being baptized with the Holy Spirit (1:4, 8).

3. Luke 3:1-17 included more contextual information than found in Matthew or Mark. Luke 3:1, 2 places John within the historical context of Tiberius Caesar, Pontius Pilate, Herod the tetrarch, and Annas and Caiaphas as high priests. In other words, the powers of the Ro-

man and Jewish worlds are identified. But, and this is a significant "but," *the word of the Lord came to John the son of Zacharias in the wilderness.* For 400 years since the book of Malachi, there was an absence of the word of the Lord. But now, in John the Baptist, the Lord was speaking again clearly and definitively. Isaiah 40:3-5 is quoted with the LXX rendering of the end of Isaiah 40:5; *all flesh shall see the salvation of God.* The theme of repentance is presented more directly in Luke 3:7-14, and John's message pointed to the Messiah, the Christ, and His baptism *with the Holy Spirit and fire* (3:16).

4. John 1:6-28 places greater emphasis on the fact that John the Baptist was not the Messiah but was the forerunner who announced the Messiah. In 1:19-23, Jewish leaders interrogated John about his identity. He made it clear that he is the one prophesied by Isaiah 40:3, *the voice of one crying in the wilderness: Make straight the way of the Lord.* The Gospel writer concluded this season by geographically placing John in the wilderness on the other side of the Jordan River.

. . . TO SERMON

A preacher could easily preach all four Advent Sundays just from Isaiah 40 and the preparation themes related to John the Baptist and Jesus. I suggest that as you develop preaching points, you keep a list of them that you can return to for preaching in the coming year. I encourage you to make certain that as you develop your message that you keep the coming of Jesus and preparation for His coming as a key theme. The gospel is the good tidings that bring hope to everyone living exiled from God. The good news is not Isaiah or John the Baptist. The good news is Jesus!

Having reminded you of the focus of preaching, let's examine some of the ways you can develop Isaiah 40 and the Gospel passages cited earlier.

1. You can approach the congregation from the standpoint that there are people living in spiritual exile. Don't assume that the "saints in the pew" are not battling their own temptations and even hidden rebellion against God. This is where you can speak about the distinction between sins and transgressions as specific acts of rebellion against God and the reality of our fallen nature as evidenced in the word *iniq-*

uity. This message can focus on holiness and sanctification as a way of entering into Advent with a deeper sense of the Holy Spirit, preparing our hearts for what the Lord wants to do in and through us.

2. Using the first idea above, you can connect this to what John the Baptist said about the baptism of Jesus. Our Lord's baptism is with the Holy Spirit and fire. The idea of "holy fire" is a powerful theme of purity and consecration that can be emphasized in this sermon. This stands in sharp contrast to the public displays of lights and holiday themes that bring us some degree of joy but often do little to impact how we live. Jesus is the Light of the world, and His fire not only purifies but enables us to be seen as His faithful witnesses.

3. Another approach is to focus on the "speaking" and "Word of the Lord" in Isaiah 40:2, 8. This can be connected directly to John 1 and the emphasis on the Word being made flesh and dwelling among us. The power of the Word of God can be expanded upon in light of Hebrews 4:11-13. But as you focus on the Word, do not forget the remainder of Hebrews 4:14-16 which addresses how the Word works in our lives as Jesus enables us to *come boldly to the throne of grace*.

4. The theme of *good tidings, the gospel* found in Isaiah 40:9, can be connected to the message and ministry of Jesus in Mark 1:14, 15 about the content of the gospel: the kingdom of God. You should note that the *gospel* does not begin with the ministry of Jesus. The *gospel* has its roots throughout the Old Testament. Two New Testament writers refer to the *gospel* being preached in the era of the Old Covenant. Hebrews 4:2 indicates that the gospel was preached to the children of Israel while they wandered in the wilderness. They were the Israelites who refused to believe God's promise of provision. God's promises and provision were manifestations of *good tidings, the gospel*. 1 Peter 4:6 speaks of the gospel being preached to the dead, which is likely a reference to what Jesus was doing while in the grave (1 Peter 3:19ff). While Jesus' preaching of the gospel concerned the kingdom of God, the demonstration of God's righteousness in Jesus was seen in the death and resurrection of Jesus (1 Corinthians 15:3 4).

5. The exegetical section dealing with Isaiah 40:2 puts some emphasis on the meaning of *iniquity* and that word in relation to holiness. You can approach this first Sunday of Advent "preparation" theme from the

side of holiness as a way of preparing the way of the Lord. Isaiah 35:8 refers to *the Highway of Holiness*. Later in 35:10, there is the familiar passage, *the ransomed of the LORD shall return, And come to Zion with singing, With everlasting joy on their heads. They shall obtain joy and gladness, And sorrow and sighing shall flee away*. Your preaching can focus on the restorative aspects of a sanctified life. That is the power of the Word and blood of Jesus transforming us into the image of Christ, who is the image of the glory of God.

3

THE SECOND SUNDAY OF ADVENT

Isaiah 7:1-17

Do we trust the Lord, or do we trust in ourselves? Do leaders believe that God is real and trust His Word, or do leaders lean solely on financial reports, political alliances, and organizational policies? More importantly, how do we speak God's Word to ungodly leaders, especially when they reject God's clear direction?

Those questions are part of the focus of Isaiah 7. Many Christians know the Isaiah 7:14 prophecy, *the Lord Himself will give you a sign: Behold, the virgin shall conceive and bear a Son, and shall call His name Immanuel.* Announced in 734 B.C., the prophecy was fulfilled seven hundred and thirty years later with the virgin birth of Jesus (Matthew 1:18, 23; Luke 1:27-31). But the prophecy also spoke directly to a wicked ruler, Judah's King Ahaz, with the challenge that God is with us, and we can depend on Him.

Historical and Literary Context

Isaiah 7 contains descriptive and conversational language between Isaiah and Judah's King Ahaz.[37] 2 Kings 16:1-20 and 2 Chronicles 28:1-27 describe his ungodly reign. Since Ahaz became king when he was twenty years old, it is likely that Isaiah, who began prophesying in 742, was only a few years older. Ahaz died when he was thirty-six years old.

Ahaz was described as a Judean ruler who "did not do what was right in the sight of the Lord his God . . . but he walked in the way of the kings of Israel." He is further described "in the time of his distress King Ahaz became increasingly unfaithful to the Lord. This is that King Ahaz. For he sacrificed to the gods of Damascus, which had defeated him, saying, 'Because the gods of the kings of Syria help them, I will sacrifice to them that they may help me.' But they were the ruin of him and of all Israel" (2 King 16:2, 3, 2 Chronicles 28:22, 23).[38]

It is the early years of Ahaz's reign (734-732 B.C.) that are the background to Isaiah 7, 2 Kings 16, and 2 Chronicles 28. Under Tiglath-pileser III (745-727 B.C.), the Assyrian Empire had grown. With its capital in Nineveh, the empire stretched from modern northern Iraq westward into southeast Turkey, northern Syria, and into northern Egypt, ultimately bringing Damascus and the twelve tribes of Israel and Judah under its control.[39]

The godlessness of Ahaz, and the disdain and frustration it caused Isaiah in Isaiah 7:13, are described in both 2 Kings 16 and 2 Chronicles 28. 2 Kings reveals the dramatic apostasy of Ahaz in building an altar in Solomon's Temple like the altar of Tiglath-pileser III found in Damascus, Syria. That the priests in Jerusalem accommodated this apostate demand of Ahaz shows the magnitude of spiritual collapse in the priesthood. Furthermore, Ahaz moved the bronze altar from its established position and used it as an idol by which he would inquire of pagan gods for direction (2 Kings 16:15). This is particularly telling in that Ahaz's grandfather, Uzziah, had attempted to worship the Lord in his own way and was struck with leprosy (2 Chronicles 26). In the instance of Uzziah, divine judgment came upon one man and not the nation. But in Ahaz, judgment came upon the nation because of his utter godlessness.[40]

2 Chronicles 28 gives greater detail to the geo-political problems faced by Ahaz as Assyria threatened the entire area. In that chapter, a military campaign is described where Judah was soundly defeated by Damascus and then brutally defeated by the Israelite king Pekah. In a massive battle, Pekah killed 120,000 Judean soldiers, including key members of Ahaz's government and household. Another 200,000 Judean women and children were taken captive to Samaria, the capital of the northern kingdom.

The slaughter in that battle was so violent that a Northern Kingdom prophet named Obed rebuked Pekah for his outrageous violence in the campaign. Obed's message was heeded by Israelite leaders, and the captives were returned to Judah.

Syria (called Damascus in these biblical texts) and the Northern Kingdom of Israel conspired to resist the encroaching Assyrian dominion. They wanted Ahaz and Judah to join their resistance confederacy. To Ahaz's credit, he chose not to join them. But instead of trusting in the Lord, as he was advised to do by Isaiah, Ahaz chose to trust in Tiglath-pileser III, the Assyrians.

All of this is the backdrop to Isaiah 7. It is a backdrop of international intrigue, threats, political alliances, military conquests and defeats, political humiliation, and a desperate game of political alliances and religious accommodation.

FROM TEXT . . .

Isaiah 7:1, 2 - The narrative begins with the historical statement that the king of Syria, Rezin, and the king of Israel, Pekah, are in alliance against Jerusalem.[41] This invasion probably occurred in 734 B.C.

It is possible that the military defeat described in 2 Chronicles 28 occurred during this campaign, though the combined armies of Syria and Israel "could not prevail against it" (Isaiah 7:1). This means that they failed in their effort to force Ahaz to join their rebellion against Assyria.

It also means that Isaiah 7:1 describes another joint effort of Syria and Israel to force Judean compliance. The statement in verse 2 reveals the serious threat facing Judah. When news came that "Syria's forces are deployed in Ephraim," it meant that Judah was again confronted with two enemies.[42]

The prophetic disdain Isaiah had towards Ahaz is revealed in 7:2 where the prophet does not even call the king by his own name. Isaiah honors the prophetic promise to the "house of David," something he repeated in 7:13 in the direct confrontation with Ahaz. Ahaz and "his people" were filled with fear. Their hearts were shaking like tree limbs in a strong wind. This metaphor describes an inability for stability and trust in the Lord.

Isaiah 7:3-6 - The Lord gave Isaiah specific instructions on what he should do and say to Ahaz. As a court prophet, Isaiah was keenly aware of the threat, the fearful atmosphere in the city, and what Ahaz was doing.

The king was inspecting the aqueduct to make sure that Jerusalem's water supply was secure if a siege occurred. The likely location of this encounter was in the southeast corner of Jerusalem. The Fuller's Field was a location where clothes were washed, and wool was prepared for use as clothing.

Isaiah took his son Shear-Jashub with him on this encounter. The son's name was prophetic, "a remnant shall return." This was not a situation where Mrs. Isaiah said, "I need a few minutes alone. Please take this child with you so I can get some peace and quiet!" This was an intentional act by Isaiah whereby the son was an object lesson to an ungodly ruler. The word *Jashub* is a noun from the Hebrew שוב (*shub* with a soft b) and means *return*. It is used extensively in the Old Testament, often translated *repent*. The presence of Isaiah's son was a warning to a rebellious king to repent and return to the ways of the Lord. The name also meant that judgment was going to come upon the nation, and only a remnant would return.

You should also observe that the idea of a *remnant* and *return* is found in Isaiah's call in 6:10, 13. Isaiah's temple call occurred about 740 B.C., and the call included the dire warning that his messages would not be heeded. That is exactly what occurred in the Isaiah 7 encounter with Ahaz.

The word of the Lord through Isaiah to Ahaz was specific: *Take heed, and be quiet; do not fear or be fainthearted for these two stubs of smoking firebrands, for the fierce anger of Rezin and Syria, and the son of Remaliah.* The son of Remaliah is Pekah of the Northern Kingdom, whom Isaiah refused to call by name. A series of imperatives to Ahaz dominate the prophetic word. To *take heed* means to pay attention. To *be quiet* means to stop listening to other voices and trying to talk yourself into an action or attitude contrary to God's voice and heart. For the first time in the passage, the word *fear* appears, though the response in 7:2 reveals that fear was the dominating emotional response to the crisis.

The Syrian and Israelite leaders thought of themselves as flaming torches about to consume Judah. They were boisterous, making themselves appear more than they were. Ahaz viewed them as a fire that would consume Judah. Isaiah viewed them from God's perspective: they were already burned out and were nothing more than whiffs of smoke from a stub.

These stubs of smoke were nothing more than hot air. Their announced goal in this invasion was to remove Ahaz and set up another king in Judah who would cooperate with their rebellion against Assyria. The alternative king was only identified as being "the son of Tabel" (7:6).[43]

Isaiah 7:7-9 - Isaiah continued speaking the prophetic Word of the Lord to Ahaz. Verse 7 contains two Hebrew negatives: *"not stand and not become"* (literally). Reinforcing the smoldering firebrand image of 7:4, Isaiah prophesied that within sixty-five years, both Syria (Damascus) and Ephraim (Israel) would fall (7:8). Within two years of this prophecy, Assyria conquered Syria (732 B.C.). The judgment upon the Northern Kingdom, Israel/Ephraim, was even more marked: "it will not be a people" (7:8). That occurred in 722 when the Northern Kingdom of ten tribes was scattered and remain so to this day.

The conclusion of 7:9 stands out and forms the basis for Isaiah's challenge to Ahaz in the following verses. Another dual use of Hebrew negatives occurred in the phrase, *"If you will not believe, surely you shall not be established."* Isaiah called Ahaz to believe the prophetic word that both Syria and Ephraim would not last. The prophet's use of the negative, *"if you will not believe . . ."* implies Isaiah's lack of confidence in Ahaz's ability to discern the promise of God. The words *believe* and *established* are from the same Hebrew word, אמן (*aman*).[44] To fail to *believe* God's word is to fail to be *established* or made firm in relation to that word.

Isaiah 7:10-12 - Merciful and patient as He is, God reached out to Ahaz again and encouraged the king to *"ask a sign for yourself from the Lord your God; ask it either in the depth or in the height above."* God patiently invited Ahaz to appeal to Himself for a confirming sign in the heavens or in the depths of the earth or sea.

But Ahaz replied with his own double negative in 7:12, *"not ask, not test the Lord."*

Isaiah 7:13-17 - One can literally hear Isaiah's frustration in his response to Ahaz. Isaiah still refused to call the king by his name or title and referred to him as the *"house of David."* Isaiah, as God's prophet, was treated with unbelieving contempt by Ahaz in his refusal to believe the Word of the Lord. Isaiah said that he himself was weary of dealing with the unbelieving king. That was one thing, but to *"weary my God also"* was far more damaging to Ahaz and the nation (7:13). This was another way of saying to Ahaz, "I'm tired of dealing with you, and God is too!"

It is here that the prophecy of the Virgin Birth enters the mind of Isaiah. Ahaz had the opportunity to ask God for a confirming sign in the realm of nature, a realm that the king could verify. But Ahaz refused to do so. Therefore, God Himself, weary of unbelieving leaders, determined to give a miraculous sign so great that only God Himself could perform it: "*Behold, the virgin shall conceive and bear a Son, and shall call His name Immanuel*" (7:14).

The connection to the account of the virgin Mary in Matthew 1 and Luke 1, 2 is obvious. But as shall be developed in the next section, attention needs to be paid to the Son who is mentioned. Walter Brueggemann rightly points out the contrast between the first son mentioned in the text, Isaiah's son named "a remnant shall return," and this second Son named "God is with us."[45] The emphasis lies upon the Son, who, by the time he is old enough to eat "curds and honey" and to know the difference between good and evil, both Syria and Ephraim will have been destroyed by Assyria (7:15, 16).

The section closed with the divine warning of impending judgment upon Judah through the instrument of Assyria, and that judgment will be as decisive as when Ephraim (Israel) separated from Judah under Jeroboam (1 Kings 12-14, 2 Chronicles 10, 11). Just as that division in 922 B.C., nearly two hundred years earlier, could not be healed, so the tragedy coming upon the Northern Kingdom would also be of a similarly permanent nature in history.

. . . TO SERMON

As we review Isaiah 7, our thoughts turn to the Virgin Birth of Jesus. His birth is truly Immanuel, *God with us*.[46] We know from Matthew and Luke that the Child conceived by the Holy Spirit would be named *Jesus*, a Greek form of the Hebrew name *Joshua*. While *Jesus* was His given name, He fulfilled the Isaiah prophecy as *God with us*; God incarnated as a fully human, yet sinless, person.

Martin Luther wrote about the name Immanuel: "This describes what kind of person it will be. This is not a proper name. He is indeed the Son of a virgin, and yet He is 'God with us,' therefore God and man."[47] John

Wesley expressed the same thought as Luther: "God dwelling among us, in our nature (John 1:14). God and man meeting in one person, being a mediator between God and men. For the design of these words . . . describe His nature and office."[48]

Rev. Noel Brooks, a significant theologian of the International Pentecostal Holiness Church, wrote, "Why was the Virgin Birth necessary? Because the Incarnation of God in human nature was a unique event, and Christ was a unique Person; therefore, His entrance into our world must be unique. Also, there must be no transmission of the taint and power of sin. An ordinary birth would have entailed a sinful nature. Through the Virgin Birth, involving a specially sanctified and prepared person, sin was excluded, and a perfect, sinless child was conceived."[49]

The Apostles' Creed, one of the earliest Christian confessions, includes this phrase, "I believe . . . in Jesus Christ, (God's) only Son, our Lord; Who was conceived by the Holy Spirit; Born of the Virgin Mary." The Virgin Birth signifies that the eternal, sinless Son of God became fully human to make atonement for Adam's sin and, through His shed blood, remedy the sin-bought separation between humanity and God.

Here are other ways to approach Isaiah 7 as a pastor addressing the needs of one's flock.

1. The contrast between Isaiah and Ahaz is startling. One is a person of faith who believes in the power of God. The other, Ahaz, is a person who looks at possibilities through the lens of human understanding and power. 2 Corinthians 5:7 addresses these two types of people, *"For we walk by faith, not by sight."* Connected to this thought is the use of *aman* in Isaiah 7:9. I refer you to 2 Chronicles 20:20, where a different Judean king, Jehoshaphat, does believe the Word of the Lord (20:14-17) and exhorts the people to believe and be established! Note that in 2 Chronicles, the negatives of Isaiah 7:9 were not used. Both Ahaz and Jehoshaphat faced overwhelming enemies and obstacles. One refused to trust God and trusted only in himself; the other did trust God and gained the victory. Proverbs 5:6 and 7 come to mind as we consider what it means to trust the Lord and lean upon Him.

2. Further development related to Ahaz is possible in light of his obstinate refusal to trust the Lord. You can develop this in terms of Ahaz

looking for "his best option" in Assyria. In the natural, his strategy makes sense. But it is not the way of faith for the people of God. Psalm 20:7 captures this difference: *"Some trust in chariots, and some in horses; But we will remember the name of the Lord our God."* This verse is an excellent segue to the power of the "name of the Lord" as the One with us.

3. Another preaching approach from Isaiah 7 relates to the question of signs. In the Isaiah 7 passage, God offered Ahaz an opportunity for a confirming sign. In what appears to be a response of false humility in Isaiah 7:12, Ahaz rejects the divine offer. I suggest you tackle the issue of "signs" carefully, as Jesus warns about a generation that seeks signs but does not seek Him (Matthew 12:39). Yet the Gospel of John refers to the "signs" that Jesus did that revealed His glory (John 2:11, 4:54). In the Bible, genuine signs are meant to draw us to the saving power of God. That was God's intention in the invitation to the apostate Ahaz.

4. Brueggemann's insight about the two sons mentioned in Isaiah 7 is interesting. Isaiah's son, "a remnant shall return," is rightly named considering divine judgment. But the last word of the gospel is not judgment; it is salvation because there is a promised Son whose name means "God is with us." Several years ago, I heard teacher Leonard Sweet remark that *"with* is God's middle name." There is much you can develop under the idea of God being "with us": Jesus *with* the disciples on the stormy sea (Mark 6:45-52); Jesus *with* the hungry masses and feeding them (Mark 6:30-44); Jesus stopping to be *with* a woman who reached out to touch Him (Mark 5:21-34).

5. Another area of consideration in the Isaiah 7 passage is the power of divine patience and longsuffering. Ahaz is a wicked man, yet God did not give up on him. In the end, it is Ahaz who gave up on God. The Christmas message is truly good news for people alienated from God. The Lord, our God, has not given up on us and continually reaches out to us to trust in His saving word. Ahaz's excuses amount to nothing in light of the great mercy that God wanted to show through him. Faith from Ahaz would have saved the nation. The faith of a sinner opens the door for transformation and change for a host of family members and friends

4

THE THIRD SUNDAY OF ADVENT

Isaiah 9:1-7

We live in a time when conspiracies and fake news have equal footing with truth and certainty. Alas, it is not a new phenomenon. The historical context of Isaiah 9, which continues from Isaiah 7 and 8, gives a divine perspective on the intellectual and moral confusion of Isaiah's time and our own.

Historical Context

The Assyrian crisis that dominates much of Isaiah 1-39 began in 745 B.C. as the new empire expanded from the Tigris and Euphrates rivers westward towards the Mediterranean Sea and southward towards Egypt. News of conquest, threats of war, and political uncertainty marked the beginnings of Isaiah's ministry in 740 B.C.

As we saw in Isaiah 7, the Assyrian advance caused political pressures as neighboring nations sought to hold off the rising tide of the growing empire. Isaiah 8 is important for our understanding of Isaiah 9 as the eighth chapter describes the political and religious atmosphere of threatened nations, particularly that of the northern and southern kingdoms of Israel and Judah. Ahaz was the Judean king, and in Isaiah 9, the prophet continued to elaborate on the nature of the Messianic deliverer promised as "Immanuel, God with us" in 7:14.

An overview of the salient points of Isaiah 8 provides the introduction to Isaiah 9.

First, 8:1-10 continued the narrative found in Isaiah 7 and referenced the birth of a second son to Isaiah and his prophetess wife (8:1-3).[50] The son was named Maher-Shalal-Hash-Baz, which means "speed to the spoil." The child's name indicated the speed of the Assyria conquest. The Lord instructed Isaiah to give this prophecy in a public, written form, witnessed by Uriah and Zechariah.[51] The birth and growth of this child paralleled the timeline related to the Immanuel prophecy of 7:15, 16, as it pertained to the Assyrian conquest.

The historical context for Isaiah 8 is essentially the same as Isaiah 7.[52] If Judah had trusted in the Lord, she would have experienced the Assyrian conquest like calm and peaceful waters (8:6).[53] Instead, Ahaz's reliance upon the spirit of the world left Judah sinking as the Assyrian military was compared to a great flood (8:7). This "military flood" would cover Israel and Judah who were called by God "Immanuel" (8:8). God's people, birthed through Abraham's faith, delivered at the Exodus, and given the Torah through Moses, were meant to be "God with us" as witnesses to the world. Their failure to so live meant the loss of their divine purpose and the loss of divine blessings to all nations.

Yet, this judgment word concluded with divine hope for restoration in 8:9, 10. The Lord promised that the "far countries" would fail. Notice the repetition of "Gird yourselves, but be broken in pieces" at the end of verse 9. The repetition emphasized the reality of God's promise, which concluded with the second use of "Immanuel, God with us," at the end of verse 10.

Isaiah 8:11-22 contains the Lord's words to the prophet himself. The Lord "spoke . . . with a strong hand," which is another way of expressing the burden and weight Isaiah felt as he was instructed that he must "not walk in the way of this people."

The "way of this people" is first characterized as "a conspiracy" (8:12). The conspiracy motif described the utter failure of explaining the Assyrian crisis. Isaiah 8:13-15 was the Lord's direct word to Isaiah to "hallow and fear" Him. The "Lord of hosts" (Hebrew: Lord Sabaoth) was Isaiah's "sanctuary" (a reference to the temple experience in Isaiah 6). However, to the unbelieving, the Lord is "a stone of stumbling and a rock of offense." This language is quoted in Romans 9:33 and 1 Peter 2:8.

In response to "the way of this people," Isaiah instructed the faithful remnant to "bind up the testimony, seal the law among my disciples" (8:16-18; it's clear from this reference that a "school" had already formed around Isaiah). Gathering around the Word provided the basis for waiting and hoping in the Lord (8:17). Isaiah 8:18a is quoted in Hebrews 2:13 as how Jesus described His followers, particularly those He had sanctified (Hebrews 2:10-13).

The second characterization of the "way of this people" is found in 8:19-22. In their confusion, the people turned to "mediums and wizards." This was a reminder in Israel's history of their first king, Saul, whom the Lord rejected for the same reasons.[54] The way to "reject" the false "way of this people" was "to the law and to the testimony" (8:20). Notice the significant qualifying phrase of 8:20bc, "If they (that is, anyone) do not speak according to this word, it is because there is no light in them." 8:20c introduced the "light," which leads to the "darkness" motif of 8:22 and Isaiah 9. Note that the failure to obey "the law and the testimony" leads to destruction, which includes loss of trust in leadership and in God and, ultimately, idolatry.

FROM TEXT . . .

Isaiah 9:1, 2 – Be sure to read Isaiah 8:21, 22 as we examine Isaiah 9. Remember, when Isaiah was written, there were no chapter and verse divisions, so readers would naturally read from Isaiah 8 straight into Isaiah 9. The Hebrew reader would have picked up immediately on the flow of poetic language in 8:22 and 9:1. For instance, *gloom* appears in both verses and reveals that the northern tribes of Zebulun and Naphtali were under the dominion of Assyria.[55]

But Isaiah 9 begins with a contrast from the close of Isaiah 8: *nevertheless*, in Hebrew, two words: כי לא pronounced *ki lo*. Two little words with profound greatness from God! Isaiah is either looking back or is looking forward prophetically to the time when the Assyrian crisis will end. The people of Galilee have lived "in darkness" due to the corruption of the Northern Kingdom and Assyrian occupation. For them, it has been as if they are dwelling "in the land of the shadow of death" (9:2). But it is upon these very helpless and hopeless people that "a great light . . . has shined."

Isaiah 9:3-5 – It is the Holy One of Israel, Lord Sabaoth, who intervened to "multiply the nation, increased its joy, broken the yoke of the oppressor off the shoulder" (9:3, 4). The magnitude of the victory is compared to the victory of Gideon over the Midianites in Judges 7. In both instances, God intervened in a helpless situation with less than courageous leaders. The reference to sandals is a metaphor meaning that an enemy has been totally defeated and is no longer a threat.

Isaiah 9:6, 7 – The source of the victory is the promised Child from Isaiah 7:14. God's act of deliverance occurs in the midst of human life and history – a child is born. Furthermore, this child is "a Son" given to us. This is the Son of God, the Messiah of Israel, prophesied and born in human history nearly 700 years after Isaiah received this prophecy.

Isaiah 9:4 mentioned two metaphors of Assyrian oppression: "yoke of burden; staff of his shoulder." These metaphors described oppressive taxes and other policies compelled by governments. This is why in 9:6, the metaphor of "shoulder" is repeated (same Hebrew word, *shekem*, שכם), and the contrast is made that the "government will be upon His shoulder" (9:6). The word *government* denotes dominion, rule, authority. Instead of an oppressive yoke on the shoulder of God's people, the government will rest upon the shoulders of the Messianic ruler. This metaphor is one of the Old Testament metaphors behind Jesus' saying in Matthew 11:29, 30.[56] The contrast between the two types of "shoulders" is intentional.

From the strength and stability of the Messiah's shoulders, His name is further identified as "Wonderful, Counselor, Mighty God, Everlasting Father, Prince of Peace (9:6). The four points below provide insight into each of these names:

1. "Wonderful counselor" is two Hebrew words, and most commentators view them as modifying the other; thus, the English comma is unnecessary. One can translate these words as "a wonder of a counselor" or "counselor of wonder."[57] The idea of "counselor" is not a term for therapy; rather, it is a term denoting someone functioning as an outstanding and wise leader. We could translate that the Messiah is a "Minister of government affairs," or liken him to a "Prime Minister." But in the case of Jesus, the language of "King" is typical, for Jesus refers to the "kingdom of God." The word *wonder* also carries the notion of singularity; that is, there is none other like Him.

2. "Mighty God" refers to the power of the Son and His eternal relationship to the Heavenly Father.

3. "Everlasting Father" refers to the eternal nature of the Son in His capacity in fulfilling the will of the Father.

4. "Prince of Peace" carries the sense of the Messiah as the ruler who brings about and maintains God's shalom (peace) on earth as it is willed in heaven.

Isaiah 9:7 continued the implications of the Messianic ruler for the earth. The Messiah's divine government will increase without limit and will establish eternal peace for all creation. The "throne of David" is more than an affirmation of God's purposes for Israel. It affirms that Israel's purpose as a blessing to the entire world will one day be fulfilled. The verse concludes with the powerful phrase, "the zeal of the Lord of hosts will perform this." God is Lord over His divine "army, hosts," which serves His purpose of establishing His eternal kingdom. This is not an invitation for the formation of manmade armies seeking to dominate the world in the name of God. Rather, it is affirmation that God's divine zeal, or jealousy to see His will fulfilled, will be accomplished in the power of God's spiritual realm made manifest in the world.

. . . TO SERMON

1. The preacher can dialogue in this passage with Isaiah 7, 8, and 9 in relation to the children that are named. Isaiah's two sons, "a remnant shall remain," and "speed the spoil," stand in contrast with the Child named Immanuel. Isaiah's sons demonstrate the way of the world: survival of the fittest (remnant) and surviving against overwhelming odds. They demonstrate the strong taking advantage of the weak. But the promised Child is revealed by the titles in 9:6: Wonderful Counselor, Mighty God, Everlasting Father, Prince of Peace.

2. Further dialogue between Isaiah 8 and 9 can be developed as you look at how the people of Israel and Judah sought revelation and comfort in "conspiracies" and "mediums and wizards" (8:12, 19). The answer to such futile thinking is in the phrase, "to the law and to the testimony" (8:20). The "law" is *Torah* and denotes the full revelation that

God has given in His Word. In Isaiah's time, that would have included everything from the Ten Commandments to the other stipulations granted to Moses in Exodus through Deuteronomy and the revelation given to the prophets. The "testimony" was more specific in that it usually indicated the "ten words" on the tablets given to Moses at Sinai; that is, the Ten Commandments. The "testimony" was the foundational statement of God's divine will. That foundation remains to this day and has been fulfilled in the person of Jesus the Messiah. As you develop this from Isaiah 8, you can draw a contrast between living under the "principalities and powers of the world" (John 14:30; Ephesians 2:2; 3:10; 6:12; Colossians 2:15; 1 Peter 3:22) and living by the power and presence of Christ and the Holy Spirit (Matthew 4:4; Romans 8:L14; 12:2; 2 Corinthians 5:7; Galatians 2:20; 5:16-25; Ephesians 2:10; 4:1-6; 5:8, 15, 16; Colossians 3:16; 1 John 2:6).

3. Directly from Isaiah 9, the preacher can pay attention to verses 1-5 and the hope that forsaken people have in the Messiah. The plight of Zebulun and Naphtali correspond to the burdens that many people experience. Some experience oppression from human governments. But the idea of government, that is, the idea that someone or something has control and dominion over you, is what stands behind the reality of our being enslaved to sin (see Romans 6). That is emblematic of darkness, distress, and gloom. But the Light has come into the world (John 1:4-9; 3:19, 21; 8:12, 9:5). You can compare our sense of hopelessness with Gideon in Judges 6, 7. We are indeed helpless apart from the power of the Lord.

4. Another approach the preacher can take related to Isaiah 9:1-5 is, after describing the hopelessness of those bound in such oppression as described in the text, to take the "nevertheless" insight from the exegesis of the *ki lo* in Hebrew. That is, show that these two simple Hebrew words are the hinges upon which the "door of nevertheless" swings from sin and death into life and freedom. You can connect this to the episode in John 8:1-12, the story of Jesus and the woman caught in adultery. This woman is under oppression of sin, manipulation by men, condemnation, and imminent death penalty. Jesus stepped into this scene and became her "nevertheless." It is significant that John 8:12 follows the episode with Jesus declaring Himself, "I am the light of the world."

5. Isaiah 9:6, 7 gives the preacher much to draw from in terms of the "governing" power of the Messiah over our lives. The discussion of "shoulders" in the exegesis can be developed in terms of Christ's authority over us. Matthew 11:29, 30 is a good connection to describe the care and tenderness of Jesus. I want to warn us to be careful that in this idea of "government," we do not allow our national political issues to define how we view Christ in the world. This is true for both religious right and religious left adherents. Both can easily fall into a form of "Christian nationalism" that is idolatrous and veils of hidden agendas that are ultimately demonic in nature. That being said, the preacher can nonetheless speak with biblical authority about the Messiah and the promise of His reign. The titles in 9:6 can each be developed as a full sermon.

As a final thought, keep in mind that preaching from the Old Testament has several steps. One, interpret the text in its historical context. Two, see if the text is specifically cited in the New Testament and prayerfully consider its usage there. For example, the Immanuel passage is used in the birth narrative in Matthew 1, or Isaiah 8:14, and the stone of stumbling is used by the Apostles Paul and Peter (Romans 9:33; 1 Peter 2:8). Three, ask how the text reveals the person and work of Christ. That may be Jesus as the deliverer, or it may reveal something about Jesus Himself and His nature (e.g., Isaiah 9:6 and the divine titles). Fourth, prayerfully ask the Holy Spirit to guide you in discerning His purposes through these texts as the Word of the Lord to you and to your flock. As in all good preaching, this means you prayerfully prepare with time to reflect, pray, seek good illustrations, and be clear about your main point(s).

THE FOURTH SUNDAY IN ADVENT

5

Isaiah 11:1-16

This Sunday concludes the four Sundays of Advent. The next Sunday is either Christmas Sunday or Christmas Day (every several years, they are the same). When I pastored, one of my favorite services of the year was the Christmas Eve Candlelight Service. All the Advent candles had been lit, and the large white candle, the Christ candle was lit in that service. Because it was Christmas Eve and families were very busy, it normally began at about 6 p.m. and concluded at about 7 p.m. After the service, excited children and adults lingered, wishing one another "Merry Christmas."

I was always aware that for my congregants, this service had all the emotions of life. For newlyweds and new parents, it was a joyful and exciting Christmas. For those who had lost loved ones, it was a Christmas of sadness.

In terms of those facing loss, I always thought of the American Civil War song, "The Vacant Chair." Originally a poem by Henry Washburn, it was written after the Battle of Ball's Bluff on October 21, 1861, when Union forces were defeated near Leesburg, Virginia, northwest of Washington D.C. Washburn was visiting the family of a Union Lieutenant who was killed in the battle. Later, George Root composed the music. The haunting lines of "The Vacant Chair" captured the sorrow that many felt and feel, "We shall meet but we shall miss him. There will be one vacant chair. We shall linger to caress him while we breathe our ev'ning prayer."[58]

From the standpoint of a pastor, it is important to remember the breath of emotions that converge in our pews Sunday after Sunday, especially during holidays.

Historical Context

In our study of Isaiah for Advent, most of our focus has been on the Assyrian crisis that began in 745 and lasted until the 680s B.C. Remember that Isaiah's ministry probably began about 740, five years after the Assyrian Empire began to exert its domination over the Middle East. It was 732 when Syria (Damascus) fell to Assyria, and ten years later, in 722/1, when the Northern Kingdom of Israel (Samaria) fell. The period from 735 to 732 is often called the Syro-Ephraimite crisis.[59]

There is little in Isaiah 11 from which to date this chapter other than within the broad scope of the Assyrian crisis. But we get some hints in Isaiah 10 where cities conquered by Assyria are named: Calno, Hamath, Arpad, and the implication that Samaria has been destroyed as was Damascus (10:9). Brevard Childs wrote, "There is a general agreement regarding the dating of the conquered cities mentioned. Calno in northern Syria fell to Tiglath-pileser III in 738. Carchemish, a Hittite city, was conquered by Sargon II in 717 and Hamath in 720. Arpad was destroyed apparently twice, in 738 and 720."[60]

Based on the cities named and the specific reference to the Northern Kingdom, Isaiah 10 and 11 probably reflect a period near the end of Ahaz's reign (715) and possibly the beginning of Hezekiah's reign (715-687).[61]

In review, this means that Isaiah 6 - 11 (and much of the remainder of Isaiah 1-39) reflects the impact of the Assyrian invasion(s). This means that the Messianic promises that Isaiah saw "through a glass dimly" (1 Corinthians 13:12) were revealed over a twenty-year period from 735 to 715 B.C.

Before focusing on Isaiah 11, insights from Isaiah 10 are pertinent to the background of Isaiah 11 and for preparing sermons and teachings.

First, there are two "woes" that appear in Isaiah 10:1-19. The initial "woe" of 10:1 is a continuation of divine judgment upon the Northern Kingdom that began in 9:8. The significance of 10:1-4 is that its government has written and enforces "unrighteous decrees" that "rob the needy of justice, take what is right from the poor of My people" (10:1, 2). It is the widows and fatherless who are powerless against oppressive government policies.

The second "woe" concerns Assyria. The Bible affirms that the nations are in the hands of God. Even wicked nations serve divine purposes, and sometimes those purposes include being "the rod of My anger" against God's rebellious people (10:5). Assyria, like most empires, had entered the phase of national arrogance and self-sufficiency (10:13-15). God, who rejects the proud, will render Assyria her due, and God will exalt helpless Israel (Job 40:12; Psalm 94:2; 101:5; 119:21; 138:6; Proverbs 6:16, 17; 15:25; 16:5; Luke 1:51; James 4:6; 1 Peter 5:5).

As we saw earlier, the Northern Kingdom was destroyed by Assyria in 722. Isaiah 10:20-34 speaks of a remnant who will survive the destruction brought on by the Assyrians. We know that the ten northern tribes were scattered throughout the Assyrian Empire and, to this day, have not been reconstituted. But the promise of the Lord is that a remnant will survive and be saved. The key word is *remnant*, a word that carries us back to Isaiah 7:3 and the prophetic nature of Isaiah's son. The Lord's word to this remnant is "do not be afraid" (10:24), and the promise is for the second time connected to Gideon's victory over Midian (Judges 6-8:21 and Isaiah 9:4).[62]

Isaiah 10:27-34 contain the final words of hope that lead to Isaiah 11. Many of you have heard the expression, "the anointing breaks the yoke" (10:27). The context of that verse is God's promise that the oppressive dominion of Assyria will be broken off the "shoulder and neck" of God's people. The language of "shoulder" takes us back to Isaiah 9 and the promise of a deliverer whose dominion will be righteous and peaceful as the "government will be upon His shoulders" (9:6, 7). The Hebrew expression that is commonly preached as "the anointing breaks the yoke" is subject to some interpretive discussion. The New International Version has, "the yoke will be broken because you have grown so fat." The American Standard Version reads, "the yoke shall be destroyed by reason of fatness."

A further comment should be made about the use of "anointing oil" in some translations, such as the New King James. The Hebrew text of Isaiah 10:27 only used the word *oil* (*shemen* שֶׁמֶן) and not the usual accompanying *anointing*. But the NKJV is not wrong to insert *anointing* because *shemen* is the same word used in Exodus and Leviticus to describe the *anointing oil* that God instructed Moses to make. It is also important to remember that in Hebrew, the word translated is transliterated as *mashiach*, from whence we derive Messiah, the Anointed One.

Regardless of the translation, the verse has these clear meanings: 1) God Himself will intervene to bring deliverance; 2) God's people, oppressed like oxen in forced labor, will have the yoke that controls them broken from them; 3) God's deliverance will be miraculous and not the result of human ingenuity and effort; 4) Whether the image is that of "anointing oil," or that of the oxen's neck growing large enough to break the yoke, the idea is that something out of the ordinary occurs.

Isaiah 10:28-32 describe what appears in the natural to be an unstoppable Assyrian advance.

But Isaiah 10:27 gave the glimpse of hope that is further elaborated in 10:33, 34, that God will "lop off the bough with terror." That is, a second metaphor of victory is given: Assyria, looming like a giant tree over the world, will be cut down by the Lord. Thus, two metaphors of divine deliverance surround the natural view of power in the world.

FROM TEXT . . .

Isaiah 11:1-5 - The reference to Assyria as a great tree overshadowing the world stands in contrast to Isaiah 11:1 and the small "Rod from the stem of Jesse" and "a Branch shall grow out of his roots." Both images imply that something is almost dead, cut to the ground, with hardly anything standing upright in the world. But it reveals that the promise of deliverance in Isaiah 10:27, 33, 34 will occur though it will take faith to see it. What will be out of the ordinary is the presence and power of "the Spirit of the Lord" acting upon this small sign (11:2). There is much to further discuss about this aspect of "smallness" in the next section on preaching.

The work of the Holy Spirit in the life of the Messianic "branch" is clear:

1. The Spirit will rest upon the Messiah. See Jesus' baptism in Matthew 3:16; Mark 1:10, 11; Luke 3:21, 22; 4:17-21; John 1:29-34 (especially verse 33).

2. Jesus will have "wisdom and understanding" through the presence of the Spirit (Matthew 12:25; 13:54; 27:18; Mark 6:2; Luke 2:40, 52: 6:8; John 2:24, 25; 6:6, 61, 64).

3. Jesus will exhibit "counsel and might" in His ministry. This phrase is similar to Isaiah 9:6, where "counselor" and "mighty" are used. Here in 11:2, the same root words are combined to express that the Holy Spirit will give Jesus the "counsel" and the divine "might" He needs in every aspect of His ministry.

4. The Holy Spirit will give Jesus the "spirit of knowledge and of the fear of the Lord." This combination is found in Proverbs 1:7, 29; 2:5; 9:10).

The "fear of the Lord" theme in 11:2, continued in 11:3 as the foundation of how the Messiah would govern the peoples of the earth. The "fear of the Lord" is not a statement of anxiety or distrust; rather, it recognizes the authority of the One over all things. The Messiah, Jesus, "delights" in knowing and doing the will of His Father. Because His eyes are upon the Father, and His ears listen to His Father, Jesus judges righteously (John 5:30; 8:28, 38; 12:49, 50).

Because of this relationship Jesus has with His Father, "righteousness is the belt of His loins" and "faithfulness (is) the belt of His waist." There are not two different belts around the midsection of the Messiah; rather, this is Hebrew poetry expressing the fullness of divine righteousness and faithfulness as the Messiah reigns over the nations.

Isaiah 11:6-9 - In *The Message of Isaiah,* Barry Webb describes Isaiah 11:1-9 in this fashion: "The passage moves from his fitness to rule (1-3a) to the character of his rule (3b-5) to the ideal state of affairs that will result from his rule (6-9)."[63] These verses constitute a Messianic prophecy of the millennial age, when sin will no longer rule the earth.

Isaiah 11:10-16 - The prophet used the visual of a banner to indicate the global impact of the Messiah's ministry.[64] The Gentile world will recognize that the Messiah is the One for whom all nations have been seeking. It is important to see in 11:11-15 that it is among the Gentiles that scattered Israel (the Northern Kingdom) will come forth and find her way back into the presence of the Lord. The people God delivered in the Exodus and formed at Mount Sinai will experience full restoration, and the peace of the land of Israel will be a sign of peace for all the world (11:13).

The banner will be seen as far away as Assyria (11:16), and the return of these peoples (literally scattered around the world) will be like a highway upon which they are traveling.

. . . TO SERMON

If you have chosen to preach through Isaiah 7-11 in the first two or three Sundays of Advent, this fourth Sunday gives you an opportunity to connect the dots that are common themes:

1. *Remnant.* The idea of a holy remnant begins in Isaiah 1:9 and is reflected in Isaiah's call in 6:13 (which also prophesied the "holy seed shall be its stump"), found again in the name of Isaiah's son in 7:3, and given more specificity in 10:20-23 and into Isaiah 11. The idea of a holy remnant, or what is termed "smallness" earlier, needs to be nuanced in presentation. The idea is not that we need to isolate ourselves from engaging the world to somehow remain pure or that we are meant to simply be a small number. No, the idea is that in spite of what the powers of the world appear to be, God has a people who are willing to stand in the gap with faith, grace, love, and mercy for the sake of His name on the earth.

2. *The Birth of the Messiah/Deliverer.* Isaiah 7:14 reveals His miraculous birth, while Isaiah 9:6, 7 reveals His righteous identity, which leads to the revelation of the source of His power (the Holy Spirit) and the righteous way He will govern (11:2-5). You can approach this from the perspective that from His birth (and actually prior to His birth), Jesus had a specific mission in the world, and so also each of us has a purpose from God for the times in which we live. While our natural birth does not correspond to Jesus' Virgin Birth, the reality is that the same Holy Spirit who conceived Jesus in the womb of the virgin is the same Holy Spirit who brings about the new birth in our lives through faith. It is in recognition of our new birth that our real identity is established. As we discover our identity in Christ, we discover what it means to be filled with the Spirit and to live in such a way as the kingdom of God is revealed through us.[65]

3. *The Present Power of an Ancient Victory.* In this study, the role of Judges 6-8 is significant background in Isaiah 9:3-5 and 10:26. Gideon's victory over the Midianites is a study in self-weakness and the struggle to accept that God can really use someone like us (Judges 6). It continues as a study of how the Lord does not need massive numbers but simply a handful of people who are fully dedicated (such as a remnant and the 300 in Judges 7). It concludes with the importance of a full victory over the spiritual enemies of our lives, what the New Testament calls putting to death the works of the flesh (Romans 6:11; 8:13; 1 Corinthians 15:31; Colossians 3:5). You can apply this to the Advent season by focusing not only on the birth of Jesus, but the purpose of His birth: ". . . the Son of Man did not come to be served, but to serve, and to give His life a ransom for many (Matthew 20:28), and "There is one God and one Mediator between God and men, the Man Christ Jesus, who gave Himself a ransom for all . . . ." (1 Timothy 2:5, 6). This connects the birth of Jesus to His redeeming death on the Cross, an event two thousand years ago that has the present power to deliver and redeem.

4. *The Contrast of Worldly Power and God's Ways of Restoration.* In the exegesis of Isaiah 10:27 - 11:2, it was observed that the Lord cut down the arrogance of a worldly empire (illustrated as a great tree; see a similar illustration in Daniel 4:1-27) and replaced it with a small branch from the roots of the promises made to David in 2 Samuel 7:5-16. Connected with this is the work of the Holy Spirit, a work evidenced in Isaiah 10:27 with the anointing that breaks the yoke of bondage and the presence and power of the Holy Spirit upon the Messiah Jesus in 11:2.

5. *The Birth of Jesus is the Promise of a Future Righteous World.* Isaiah 11 is a wonderful text to speak of the future. It stands alone from human efforts to forge "a lasting peace." As long as sin has dominion over the hearts and minds of people, real peace, justice, and righteousness cannot occur. But we are not without hope. Unless the Lord returns during our lifetimes, we shall not see it this side of eternity. But the promise remains that Jesus is the "banner," the "ensign" that all the world will see. The promise in Isaiah 11 that the scattered and "lost" children of the Northern Kingdom will find their way home is

a promise made certain in the resurrection of Jesus and the promise of our resurrection from the dead.

6

CHRISTMAS DAY

Isaiah 7:14 and Matthew 1:1-25

Introduction

Christmas Day, December 25, as the observance of the birth of Christ began during the fifth century (400s A.D.). Prior to this, the birth of Christ was observed during the spring. As the church's influence grew across the Roman Empire, it competed with various political and religious entities. The most significant was the cult of Mithras. The Persian god of light, symbolized by the sun, Mithras, "promised eternal life to the brave, and became a favorite of Roman soldiers" in the eastern territories of the empire. When these soldiers returned to Rome, they came worshipping the Persian god on December 25. They gave this festival "*natalis invicti solis*, 'the birth of the unconquerable sun.'"[66]

Confronted by the continuing sexual immorality reflected in Roman culture and the impact of the idolatry gaining strength in the Roman military, the church sought to bring righteousness to the empire by substituting the idolatrous date with the righteous birth of Jesus Christ on December 25. For over 1600 years, "the mass of Christ," that is, Christmas, has been celebrated on this date.[67]

FROM TEXT . . .

The first four Sundays of Advent emphasized texts in order from Isaiah 40 and 7-11. The exegetical sections focused on the historical context of Isaiah. Considering that emphasis on Isaiah, note how verses in these chapters were cited by New Testament authors.

1. Isaiah 7:14 cited in Matthew 1:23.
2. Isaiah 8:12, 13 cited in 1 Peter 3:14, 15.
3. Isaiah 8:14 cited in Romans 9:33.
4. Isaiah 8:17, 18, cited in Hebrews 2:13.
5. Isaiah 8:23 - 9:2, cited in Matthew 4:15, 16.
6. Isaiah 11:10 cited in Romans 15:12.[68]

For Christmas Eve, a Christmas Day service, or Christmas Sunday, our study is on Matthew 1:1-25 and Isaiah 7:14.

Matthew 1:1-16 – Matthew's genealogy goes from Jesus Christ back to David and Abraham, in contrast with Luke's, which goes back to Adam. This indicates a predominately Jewish audience, or at least the importance of addressing the person of Jesus for the sake of Jews. The connection to David is a connection of Messianic promises and kingship. The promises made with Abraham, which included the nations, locates Jesus within the divine history of faith. In both David and Abraham, Jesus is connected to the Old Testament story that began in Genesis 11:10, 26. It is important to observe that the genealogy of Genesis 11:10ff begins immediately following the loss of common communication among peoples with the Tower of Babel account. The Abraham story becomes God's way to speaking to one person through whom a whole people are meant to communicate God's truth to a divided world.

As the genealogy unfolded in Matthew 1:1-17, the role of five women has often been observed: Tamar (Matthew 1:3; Genesis 38); Rahab (Matthew 1:5; Joshua 2); Ruth (Matthew 1:5; the book of Ruth); "the wife of Uriah," Bathsheba, (1:6; 2 Samuel 11); Mary, the mother of Jesus (Matthew 1:16). Under the heading, "Why Bring on the Ladies?", the late New Testament scholar Raymond Brown discussed reasons why Matthew included these women. In his commentary on the birth narratives in Matthew and Luke, Brown gave the three main explanations.[69]

The first reason, espoused by the church father Jerome (ca. 340s to 420 A.D.), was that the women were regarded as sinners and represent the mercy and forgiveness shown by Jesus as the Savior. Martin Luther is characteristic of the second reason where the first four women were identified as foreigners. Tamar and Rahab are Canaanites, Ruth is a Moabite, and Bathsheba was married to a Hittite. The main point of this interpretation is that in the gospel, the Gentile world is included beyond the Jews. The third proposal, which Brown wrote, "has considerable following today," finds that there was something extraordinary or irregular in their union with their marriage partners, and "the women showed initiative or played an important role in God's plan."[70]

Matthew 1:17 – Matthew inserted an interesting timeline between the genealogical names and the Jesus birth narrative. The first era is from Abraham to David, approximately 900 years from about 1800-900 B.C. This covers the biblical narrative from Genesis 11 to the end of 2 Samuel. While that period of Jewish history had its failures and scoundrels, it was nonetheless highlighted by Abraham's faith, God's faithfulness to fulfill His promises to Abraham, and the establishment of a unified nation under a divinely-anointed king.

The second era is from David to the Babylonian Captivity, a little over 300 years (900-587 B.C.). This period was marked by religious and political division, unfaithfulness to the Lord, and divine judgment upon Israel and Judah.

The third era is from the end of the Babylonian Captivity to the birth of Jesus, 538 to 4 B.C., about 500 years. That era marks the survival of the remnant that was so prominent in Isaiah. Following the words of post-exilic prophets like Malachi, it describes the gap when the Word of the Lord was rare for several hundred years until the eternal Word became flesh (John 1).

Matthew's use of these three eras marks out the key periods of time in Jewish history, showing a continuity of divine purpose in spite of human failure and disobedience. As Matthew 1:1 connected Jesus to Abraham and David, the three eras connect Jesus back to the same, emphasizing faith (Abraham) and righteous kingship (David).

Matthew 1:18, 19 –The birth narrative was clearly introduced with the divine name and title: "Jesus Christ." The name "Jesus" is the Greek form of Joshua, meaning "the Lord is my salvation" or "my deliverer." The title

"Christ" refers to the office of Jesus as that of the promised Messiah, the Anointed One sent by God to deliver His people.

Matthew's birth narrative is succinct compared to Luke's account. But it is filled with significance. First, 1:18 clearly affirms that Mary's pregnancy was not the result of her relationship with Joseph, ". . . before they came together." Instead, it affirms that the conception was a miraculous act of the Holy Spirit.

Joseph is identified as "her husband," which to modern readers implies they had consummated their marriage, thus negating verse 18. But that modern reading fails to understand Jewish wedding and marriage customs at the time of Christ. Marriage was a two-step process where the betrothal was a legally binding act, not only between the man and woman but between their families. It was the first step in a binding covenant that included economic transactions between the families. Thus, the groom had responsibilities to prepare a home for his wife between the engagement and the actual wedding, while the bride prepared for life outside that of the family she had known since birth. It was so binding that it took the legal step of a divorce to break the engagement.[71]

Matthew 1:19 reveals that Mary's betrothed husband was "a just man." That is, he was righteous in his heart and actions. As one would expect, he did not understand why she was with child, much less the explanation of how she was pregnant. But his righteous heart kept him from wanting to publicly divorce her ("put her away").

Matthew 1:20-23 – Not only was Joseph righteous in a personal way, as evidenced by his proposed treatment of Mary, but his righteousness made it possible for the Holy Spirit, through an angel and dream, to speak to him.

Notice the following from 1:20:

1. Joseph continued to "think, ponder" the situation with Mary. His responses were not rash or angry. No doubt, he was heartbroken, but he did not allow his emotions to control him.

2. The word *behold* (ἰδού, idou) is important. It announces that revelation is forthcoming. Matthew intentionally used this word as it was found in the Septuagint of Isaiah 7:14, which is quoted in Matthew

1:23. This word is used four times in Matthew 1:20, 23; 2:13, 19, all in relation to the revelation given to, and received by, Joseph.

3. The "dream" aspect is an intentional echo of the Old Testament figure Joseph (Genesis 37-50).[72] Just as the patriarch Joseph had divinely-ordered "dreams" (Genesis 37:5-11, 40, 41, where Joseph interprets dreams), so also did Joseph in relation to Mary and the Child (Matthew 1:20; 2:12 the Magi, 13, 19, 22). Just as the patriarch Joseph found Egypt as a place of refuge for his family during a famine crisis, so also Joseph found Egypt as a place of refuge for his family when threatened by Herod (Matthew 2:13-15, 19-23). The patriarch Joseph was "righteous" when Potiphar's wife attempted to seduce him (Genesis 39:6-12). So Joseph was righteous in regard to Mary.[73]

4. The "dream" was clearly identified as of divine origin by the reference to an angel (messenger) who "appeared" to Joseph.

5. The angelic message was crystal clear to Joseph. He was called by name and associated with the royal lineage of David. The instructions first addressed Joseph's fear, then secondly, gave specific directions and clarification regarding the origin of the Child's conception.

The divine message continued into verse 21 that the Child will be "a Son, and you shall call His name Jesus, for He will save His people from their sins." The identity of the Son's name, Jesus, is a name Joseph would have immediately connected to the Old Testament figure Joshua.

Matthew 1:22, 23 further connected the situation to Isaiah 7:14 as the fulfillment of a prophecy that was over 700 years old. The *Immanuel* prophecy of Isaiah 7 needed no further explanation to Joseph as he, like any other ancient Israelite, would have had knowledge of the Old Testament. He would have connected the prophecy to his Davidic line.

Matthew 1:24, 25 – Matthew described Joseph's response to the angelic message in terms of immediate obedience. This stands in sharp contrast to the wavering and disobedience of Ahaz, also in the Davidic line, when the Immanuel prophecy was given (Isaiah 7:10-17). Ahaz viewed his circumstances solely from the natural eye and thus missed the miraculous power of God. Joseph received the divine message and believed in the supernatural power of God.

Verse 25 showed that Mary's pregnancy had no connection to human sexual activity until after the birth of the Messiah. This was not meant to imply that human sexual activity is sinful when done in accordance with the Word of God. Rather, it shows that Joseph and Mary understood the fulfillment of the prophetic that they were called to observe in their roles as the "carriers" of the divine promise given to Abraham and to David.

. . . TO SERMON

Whether on Christmas Eve or a Christmas Day service, the preacher needs to be aware that the congregants likely are focusing on holiday activities with their families. The point is that a sermon on this day does not need to be lengthy. A well-prepared 15 to 20-minute message with clear points and strong illustrations is better suited for such an occasion. With that in mind, let's review preaching themes and directions from Matthew 1.

1. To modern people, especially those with little knowledge or even interest in Jewish history, the connection of Jesus to Abraham and David seems remote. Some may view it as a historical curiosity, others as irrelevant. But the reality is that for the kingdom of God and the salvation of the world, including the individuals sitting in our pews, these connections are essential.

    a. Abraham is a connection of God's promises with a person of faith. God's promises, and that He keeps His promises, are part of what it means that God is righteous (Romans 1:16, 17; 3:21-26; 4:1-4, 13-25).

    b. God is pleased when His children have faith in His promises (Hebrews 11:6). Such faith is a sign of trust, which is the foundation for any meaningful relationship between people and especially between us and our Heavenly Father.

    c. The promise to Abraham was that through his lineage, blessings become available for the entire world (Genesis 12:1-3 where *bless* ברך *barak* is used five times). Most individuals want to be considered a blessing to their family, their friends, and their church. The eternal weight of those blessings is discovered by living "in Christ," that is, in the Messiah.

d. Jesus is the fulfillment of the kingship promises made to Israel's King David (2 Samuel 7:12-16). Again, the foundation of righteousness is central to God's promise. We saw this in Romans 4 with Abraham. Sandwiched between the Romans 4 teaching about Abraham is the reality of the same promises and righteousness to David (Romans 4:5-8). In particular, the focus in Romans 4 with David is the reality of God's mercy to us expressed in "Blessed are those whose lawless deeds are forgiven, and whose sins are covered; blessed is the man to whom the Lord shall not impute sin" (Romans 4:7, 8 quoting Psalm 32:1, 2).

e. Finally, the connection with David as "king" provides a way to discuss the reality of the kingdom of God that is present and is coming with Jesus as the King. From the standpoint of Christmas, you can speak to the promise that the turmoil of the nations is not the final word for this world. God's kingdom one day will bring full peace, righteousness, and justice to this sin-plagued world.

2. Any one of the five women listed in Matthew 1:2-16 is a possible sermon topic for Christmas Day as each, or the whole, can be connected to Mary, the mother of Jesus. The exegetical section provided three primary interpretive models. If I were preaching on these women today, I would develop the message around the third approach mentioned by Raymond Brown.

3. The focus on Matthew's birth narrative is on Joseph. As noted in the exegesis, you could take several approaches in focusing on the response of a man in dealing with a difficult situation and listening to the voice of God (not at the exclusion of women). In particular, Matthew 1:19, 20 give characteristics of Joseph that are noteworthy: he was a righteous man, he pondered circumstances and refused to be reactionary. Instead, he allowed time for a more productive response and was able to hear and recognize the voice of God through a dream.

4. Finally, Matthew 1:23 cited Isaiah 7:14 and is an appropriate Christmas Eve or Christmas Sunday text. You can refer to the exegesis of Isaiah 7 in an earlier chapter of this book for more background. If you go in this direction, be sure to develop your sermon around the theme of "fulfilled" that is mentioned in Matthew 1:22. This can be connected to Galatians 4:4 and the birth of Jesus "in the fulness of time."

BEYOND CHRISTMAS CELEBRATIONS

THE REALITY OF EVIL IN THE WORLD AND THE TRIUMPH OF JESUS

Jeremiah 31:15; Matthew 2:13-23; Acts 6:8 - 7:60

Introduction

The Sunday after Christmas Day feels like an "in-between" Sunday between Christmas celebrations and the New Year. The focus often shifts towards January 1st, New Year's Day, unless it falls immediately after Christmas Day, in which case we can still preach on one of the major Christmas texts from Matthew or Luke.

In approaching New Year's, it is tempting to preach about starting again with fresh resolutions (most of which are seldom kept!). But I want to suggest another approach, one that keeps the congregation connected to the significance of the "why" Jesus came to earth to die and addresses the reality of sin in a fallen world and its accompanying horrors.

So, why the three texts in the heading? First, the slaughter of the Bethlehem children has a connection to Jacob's wife Rachel, who is mentioned in Jeremiah 31:15. It will be mentioned in this chapter as it is the context for the slaughter of Bethlehem's children in Matthew 2:16-18, which is the primary Gospel text for this Sunday. The passage from Acts 7 is about the death of the first Christian martyr, Stephen. In both the Western and Eastern churches, his death is remembered following Christmas Day.[74]

FROM TEXT . . .

Jeremiah 31:15 - Known as the "weeping prophet," Jeremiah lived in the dark days of the collapse of the southern kingdom of Judah. His ministry began a little over one hundred years after Isaiah. Jeremiah's prophecies began in the middle part of Josiah's reign (640-609 B.C.), probably about 627, and covered a forty-year period that included the destruction of Jerusalem by Nebuchadnezzar (587), the beginning of the Babylonian Exile, and his life in Egypt (Jeremiah 43).

Three waves of Jews were taken from Judah to Babylon. The first wave occurred in 592 because of Judea's rebellion against Babylon. It is likely that the prophet Ezekiel was taken in this group. The second wave occurred in 587 with the destruction of Jerusalem. The third occurred in 582.[75] Thus, Jeremiah's prophecies concerned the fate of these Judean leaders who had been removed to Babylon. You see this in the oft-quoted Jeremiah 29, where Jeremiah wrote a letter to the captives telling them to prepare for seventy years and giving them hope (29:11). But Judah continued to rebel against Babylon. This was something Jeremiah saw as the same as rebelling against the Lord. Following Jeremiah 29, the tone of Jeremiah's prophecies changed to reflect the growing situational despair. Though not without hope for the future and the promise of deliverance from exile, Jeremiah rightly heard "lamentation and bitter weeping, Rachel weeping for her children" (31:15).

Rachel was the wife of Jacob. Interestingly Jacob met her in "the land of the people of the East" (Genesis 29:1). He fled there to preserve his life following the deception which gained him the birthright from his brother Esau (Genesis 27). The area was known as Padan Aram, and it was where Abraham's family had gathered following their migration from Ur of the Chaldees (Genesis 28:2; 11:27-12:4). The area was north of what was later identified as the Assyrian and Babylonian Empires. Though Rachel only had two of the twelve sons of Jacob (Joseph and Benjamin), she was most loved by him (Genesis 35:23-26), and all the tribes of Israel as a nation (named after the 12 sons) became identified with her. Joseph's two sons, Manasseh and Ephraim, were associated with the Northern Kingdom, and Benjamin was associated with the Southern Kingdom alongside Judah.

By the time of Jeremiah, the northern tribes under the collective name of Ephraim had been scattered for over 120 years. Individual Jewish families likely remained and kept their identity over those years. Jeremiah and others knew of these families who kept alive God's promise that they would return to Israel one day. That promise awaits complete fulfillment.

Thus, Jeremiah 31:15, which is set almost midway through a chapter of hope and promise of a new covenant (31:31-34), stands out as a reminder of the profound suffering and loss that comes because of sin. It was a mother's pitiful cry that Jeremiah heard in his spirit as he considered the plight of all the captives. "They are no more" reflected the reality that, at best, a handful of people taken in the Assyrian Captivity remained. Like a mother who has lost her children to the grave, Rachel found no solace or comfort.

It is also important to remember that Rachel was buried near Bethlehem (Genesis 35:16-20; 48:7) as she died following the birth of Benjamin. Thus, the connection to the deaths of the Bethlehem children in the failed attempt to murder the Messiah is evident.

Matthew 2:13-15 – The setting for this account is likely eighteen to twenty-four months after the birth of Jesus. The Holy Family remained in Bethlehem and received significant financial gifts from the wise men who came "from the East."[76] It was these gifts that helped the family flee to and remain in Egypt until the threat had passed. The setting involved the political threat of Jesus to the ruling powers in Judea under the authority of Rome, that is, Herod the Great. One cannot help but notice that at His birth and again at His death, Jesus was a threat to the powers of the earth.

While the text does not say, it is reasonable to conclude that the warning dream the Magi had (Matthew 2:12) was something they shared with Joseph and Mary. After the Magi left, their warning was confirmed in a revelatory dream to Joseph. That the Holy Family fled at night indicates the urgency of escaping to Egypt (2:14). Matthew 2:15 quoted from Hosea 11:1 and Numbers 24:8 to show that this escape to Egypt was prophesied centuries prior. It also implies that Jesus, as the fulfillment of Israel's destiny, is the "new" Israel coming out of Egypt and fulfilling its destiny.

Matthew 2:16-18 – The "slaughter of the Holy Innocents" is briefly described. The horror is captured by the anger of King Herod and the quotation from Jeremiah 31:15 described above. Herod served as King of Judea under Roman rule for thirty-three years. He became the military governor of Galilee at age twenty-five. A crafty and manipulative leader, he developed relationships with Roman leaders such as Mark Antony and Octavian (who later became the emperor Augustus). He was even involved at a distance with the schemes of Antony and Cleopatra! By the year 20 B.C., he was the ruler over all the territories in ancient Israel that were under Roman rule.

Herod had great plans for the territories he ruled. He founded cities to honor the Romans, and the archeological remains at Caesarea Maritima on the Mediterranean Sea, 56 kilometers north of modern Tel-Aviv, reveal an impressive seaport and city. He built a towering fortress south of Jerusalem where he was buried, the Herodium (which can still be seen today). He rebuilt the Temple and expanded its location on the Temple Mount. The Western Wall (sometimes called the "Wailing Wall" still stands). This is the Temple that Jesus would have seen in His youth and adult ministry.

But Herod was a violent man, fearful for his position. He murdered his wife, Mariamne, and three of his sons. The account of his slaughter of boys under the age of two in Bethlehem is consistent with Herod's disposition and wrathful actions.[77]

Matthew 2:19-23 – Herod died while the Holy Family was in Egypt.[78] As word reached Joseph that Herod was dead, the Holy Spirit, in another dream, confirmed that it was safe to return to the land of Israel. The family likely planned on returning to Bethlehem in Judea, but the Holy Spirit again warned Joseph, and the family went into the region of Galilee and settled in Nazareth, the hometown of Mary and Joseph (Matthew 2:22; Luke 1:26; 2:4). The citation at the conclusion of Matthew 2:23 is difficult to trace to a specific Old Testament text. In my opinion, Raymond Brown offers a reasonable interpretation which is discussed in the footnotes.[79]

Acts 6:1-15 - Acts 6 introduced the first internal conflict within the growing Christian community in Jerusalem. Though among Jews, it revealed cultural differences between Palestinian Jewish and Hellenistic (Greek-influenced) followers of Jesus. It showed the sensitivities of various groups and the struggle to live out the call of Jesus on a practical basis. Stephen was a Hellenistic Jew who was commissioned by the apostles to be a deacon, that is, someone who served the needs of the community. He was one of seven men chosen to take care of these important social and administrative needs of the community. He fit the criteria of being a man of good reputation and full of the Holy Spirit and wisdom (Acts 6:3).

Stephen's ministry quickly expanded to sharing the Good News of Jesus with other Jews in the Hellenistic community. Acts 6:8 indicates that he "was full of faith and power" and "did great wonders and signs among the people." He quickly discerned the implications of traditional Jewish belief because of the death and resurrection of Jesus. Stephen was a forerunner of the Apostle Paul in that he understood that Jesus' life had profound meaning for the Torah (6:9-15).

Acts 6:9 reveals that the conflict arose among the Hellenistic Jews from the Synagogue of the Freedmen, in Jerusalem. The King James Version more accurately captures the Latin background of this synagogue by translating "Freedmen" as "Libertines," the Greek transliteration is *Libertinos*. This likely referred to Jews who had once been Roman slaves or were descendants of such slaves.[80]

Unable to refute Stephen effectively, the Jews brought false charges against him (6:11-14) and brought him before the Sanhedrin.

Acts 7:1-60 - This chapter is Stephen's defense before the high priest. The defense is based on Stephen using Israel's history as the way to refute the false charges. The defense began with Abraham's journey (7:2-8) and then spent most of the remainder of the defense centering on Israel's experience in Egypt and Moses as the deliverer (7:9-44). Stephen used the tabernacle in the wilderness as the link to Jesus as God's tabernacle with us (7:45-50). The rebellious nature of Israel in her history was transferred to the Jews who killed Jesus as "betrayers and murderers" (7:52).

This final step of connecting Israel's rebellious past with the recent death of Jesus led to the crowd stoning Stephen (7:54-60). The presence and role of a young Pharisee named Saul, later called Paul, is included in the concluding verses of Stephen's death.

. . . TO SERMON

The title of this chapter captures the intent of the biblical selections used for the first Sunday after Christmas. The selection of the texts from Matthew 2 and Acts 7 are ways that the church seeks to keep the secular festive Christmas activities from becoming mere myth. Stephen's martyrdom is remembered on December 26, and the slaughter of Bethlehem's children on December 28. Both dates and accounts are sharp reminders that the birth of Jesus is not about the feel-good celebrations that dominate the modern Christmas season. Rather, Jesus was born to deal with the evil and sin that enslave humanity and the power of death over human life.

The divine purpose of the Incarnation is powerfully expressed in Hebrews 2:14, 15: "Inasmuch then as the children have partaken of flesh and blood, He Himself likewise shared in the same, that through death He might destroy him who had the power of death, that is, the devil, and release those who through fear of death were all their lifetime subject to bondage."

I encourage you to avoid preaching a motivational sermon about New Year's resolutions and becoming a better person in the coming year. That is not gospel preaching; at its worst, it's a form of righteousness by works and Pelagianism.[81] Gospel preaching takes seriously the mission of Jesus and His birth and death. Christmas without Good Friday and Easter is nothing more than a watered-down form of commercial therapy, a myth serving social and economic ends. Good Friday and Easter without the reality of the Incarnation, Matthew 2 and Acts 7, is little more than the tragic death of either a misguided man or a great hero. It is imperative that our sinful, fallen condition be taken seriously for Christmas to have its biblical purpose. Thus, here are some directions you can take these texts as you prepare to preach.

1. The slaughter of the children in Bethlehem by the threatened political powers (represented by Herod) resonates significantly in our day. Even with the overthrow in the United States of the 1973 *Roe v Wade* decision that released the floodgates of abortion in the nation, the battle for future generations continues to be fought in Congress and in state legislatures.[82] The United States continues to promote and foster abortion around the world. Government efforts that lead to promoting the widespread death of future generations are a manifestation of the

spirit of death that has hovered over the earth since Adam and Eve sinned in Genesis 3.

2. While abortion on demand is an important issue, I suggest you add to it reflections on how Satan seeks to destroy young lives through multiple means. The current gender transition movement is another method Satan uses to destroy a child's capacity to procreate. But children are also destroyed by poverty, lack of educational opportunities, broken homes, drugs and alcohol, abuse at home, and sadly, abuse within the church. In many of these instances, it is more than government irresponsibility. The responsibility includes the failure of parents and, yes, even the church to make certain that children have safe environments to grow into the adults God created them to be.

3. The death of St. Stephen is a powerful reminder of the price that followers of Jesus have paid for confessing the truth. It has been estimated that more Christians were martyred in the 20th century than in all the previous 2000 years.[83] Use your internet search engine to get current information on the places where Christians are most likely to be killed for their faith today.[84] As you preach on this and on the related subject of suffering for Christ, keep in mind the Apostle Peter's admonitions: 1 Peter 3:13 - 4:6.

4. Another aspect of Matthew 2 that can be developed is how Joseph understood how to protect the Holy Child. The previous chapter discussed the significance of dreams in how Joseph (and the Magi) discerned the voice of God to protect the future. Whether through dreams, reading the Word, clear guidance from others, or learning to recognize the prompting of the Holy Spirit in our hearts, we must be alert for the things that seek to destroy those we most love in our homes.

5. Related to the paragraph above, another area you can focus on is how the gifts of the Magi provided the financial resources for the Holy Family. We are not told the amounts, but it is likely that each of the gifts (Matthew 2:11) was substantial and gave Joseph, Mary, and Jesus the resources they needed in Egypt and when they returned to Nazareth. Your message can focus on how God provides in advance for what we need in obeying His call in our lives. The English word *provide* is from the Latin *providere*. The *pro* means "before," and *vide*

means "see." God "sees before" what we will encounter and what we will need, and God provides.

8

EPIPHANY

DISCOVERING WHO JESUS IS

Matthew 2:1-11, Micah 5:2, Titus 2:11, 3:4

Introduction

"The Twelve Days of Christmas" is a popular song about a series of gifts given by "my true love." While the song dates from the late 1700s, it reflects continuing celebrations of the twelve days from Christmas Day to January 6th, the "Epiphany." The Epiphany begins with the visit of the Wise Men and the manifestation of Jesus to the Gentiles (Matthew 2).[85] The "twelve days" begins on Christmas Day and concludes on January 5th. Perhaps you have read William Shakespeare's "Twelfth Night." The title and occasion of the play is the end of the twelve days and has this memorable phrase, "Be not afraid of greatness. Some are born great, some achieve greatness, and some have greatness thrust upon them."[86]

We saw in the previous chapter that during the week following Christmas Day, the church has historically remembered the reality of sin, injustice, suffering, and martyrdom, which is part of what it means to follow Jesus. In a sense, the twelve days leading to the Epiphany are indeed times of reflecting on what "my true love," Jesus, has given us through His suffering and resurrection. Approaching Epiphany, we are invited to hear Jesus speak to us as He did the church in Ephesus, remembering our "first love" and worshipping and serving Him "in Spirit and in truth."[87]

The temptation for the preacher is to view the preaching opportunities during these days from the standpoint of popular culture; that is, finding spiritual lessons on New Year's or even in the United States, the Super Bowl, or similar sporting events. My hope is that you will take the time to engage the biblical texts presented in this chapter and use them as the basis for teaching your flock about Jesus.[88]

Before we engage the identified texts, a word about *Epiphany*; it is from a Greek word used in Titus 2:11 and 3:4, *epiphaino* (ἐπιφαίνω), which means *become visible, show unto, appear to, manifested*. In a sense, Epiphany concludes the Christmas season and begins the season of discovering that this child born in the backwater of the Roman Empire is the Son of God, the Savior of the world, the Lamb of God, and the eternal Word made flesh. If we truly believe Colossians 1:15-18, the revelation of who Jesus is constitutes the most significant "Epiphany" of our lives: "He is the image of the invisible God, the firstborn over all creation. For by Him all things were created that are in heaven and that are on earth, visible and invisible, whether thrones or dominions or principalities or powers. All things were created through Him and for Him. And He is before all things, and in Him, all things consist. And He is the head of the body, the church, who is the beginning, the firstborn from the dead, that in all things He may have the preeminence," then the revelation of who Jesus is constitutes the most significant "Epiphany" of our lives.

FROM TEXT . . .

Matthew 2:1, 2 - The visit of the Magi, the wise men, occurred sometime after the birth of Jesus. Luke 2 records several events that occurred within the first weeks of the birth of Jesus: the revelation to the shepherds on the evening of the birth (2:8-20), the circumcision of Jesus on the eighth day, and the formal giving of His name (2:21; Leviticus 12:3), and the purification of Mary and the prophecies of Simeon and Anna (2:22-38; Leviticus 12:4-8) which occurred thirty-three days after the child's circumcision.[89]

The Hebrew name *Bethlehem* means *house of bread*.[90] Located about five miles south of Jerusalem, the site is first mentioned in the Bible in Genesis 35:19 and 48:7 in connection with the burial plot of Jacob's wife, Rachel.

The village itself predates its Abrahamic family connections, though 1 Chronicles 2:42ff mentions sons named Bethlehem and apparent links to the village.[91]

The lineage of Jesse and his son David is the most well-known Old Testament figures associated with Bethlehem. However, in the era prior to the monarchy, Judges 17, 19 describes an unnamed Levite young man from Bethlehem of Judah and the tragic story of the death of his concubine, who was also from Bethlehem.[92]

The most famous Old Testament associations with Bethlehem are found in the book of Ruth, the narratives associated with David (1 Samuel 16:4; 17:12, 15; 20:6, 28; 2 Samuel 2:32; 23:14, 16, 24; 1 Chronicles 11:16-26), and the prophetic reference in Micah 5:2.

The Magi are described as coming "from the east" to Jerusalem (Matthew 2:1). That can mean Persia, Babylon, or even the Arabian or Syrian Desert. Raymond Brown provides extended discussion related to the Magi, their origins, and their beliefs.[93]

The Magi came to Jerusalem seeking "the King of the Jews . . . for we have seen His star in the east and have come to worship Him" (Matthew 2:2). The reference to the "star" not only refers to an object in the skies but also may include a reference to Balaam's prophecy in Numbers 24:17, "I see Him, but not now; I behold Him, but not near; a Star shall come out of Jacob; A Scepter shall rise out of Israel."

Numerous theories account for the unusual celestial demonstration that the Magi followed. That ancient wise men used the stars, or astrology, to navigate to Jesus was not an uncommon form of guidance. In fact, today, millions of people still use astrology as a medium for guidance, though we must remember that the Bible rejects astrology as a form of divine communication. One might interpret this portion of the Magi account as showing that the time for using idolatrous astrology has ended with the revelation of Jesus as the Messiah.[94]

Matthew 2:2 concluded with the Magi indicating the intent of their search: to kneel before this Child in worship, acknowledging that God was up to something significant in the birth of this Child. This is the first of three uses of the word *worship* in the visit of the Magi (2:2, 8, 11).[95]

Matthew 2:3-6 – The text implies that the Magi were in Jerusalem asking about the birth of the "king of the Jews" some time before word came to Herod the Great, the Roman installed "king of the Jews." At some point, word came to the royal court about the rumors of the birth of a new king. The text is clear that this was not welcomed news to the ruling political/religious parties. It was "troubling" to the king and "all Jerusalem with him" (2:3). Why would "all Jerusalem" be troubled? Because for the ruling parties, it meant a threat to their own power as well as the potential for greater Roman involvement if this was the beginning of a revolt.

Herod brought the chief priests and scribes together to ascertain "where the Christ was to be born" (2:4). Notice that the language shifted from "the king of the Jews" to "the Messiah." This was Matthew's way of re-inforcing that the Child causing this concerning news was more than a Jewish political king. This Child has a divine anointing. His life meant far more than the normal understanding of kingship.

The religious leaders searched the Scriptures and found the citation in Micah 5:2. A contemporary of Isaiah, Micah prophesied some 700 years before the birth of Jesus. It is likely he knew the Messianic prophesies of Isaiah and may have been part of a school of prophets led by Isaiah. His Messianic prophecy began in Micah 4 with a vision of "many nations shall come and say, 'Come, and let us go up to the mountain of the Lord, to the house of the God of Jacob; He will teach us His ways, and we shall walk in His paths.' For out of Zion the law shall go forth, and the word of the Lord from Jerusalem" (4:2). It is in this larger context of Israel fulfilling her divine calling as a witness to the nations that the Holy Spirit spoke to Micah concerning the promises made to David regarding the reign of One from his lineage (2 Samuel 7:8-16).

Thus, the Micah 5 reference to Bethlehem is not a random choice. It is connected to the fulfillment of a divine promise that was already two hundred years old when Micah prophesied. Matthew combined most of Matthew 5:2 with a reference from 2 Samuel 5:2: "You shall shepherd My People Israel and be a ruler over them." This reinforced Matthew's insight of Micah that it was a prophecy rooted in the promises of God to David.

Matthew 2:7, 8 – In a previous chapter in this book, I have described the utter wickedness of Herod the Great. Here we see his cacodemon nature as he "secretly" meets with the Magi with an ulterior motive. The priests and scribes, and other members of the court are not present at this meeting. It is manipulative, as he does not want anyone else to know what he is doing. His instructions were clear to the Magi, and he was counting on them to do what he demanded.

Matthew 2:9-12 – Tradition has led to the view that there were three wise men.[96] That view is based on the assumption that the three gifts of gold, frankincense, and myrrh were given to the Holy Family by three different people. In reality, there is no defense for that view, and it is likely that the wise men were accompanied by others for protection and accommodation on their journey to Jerusalem and Bethlehem.

The "star" which led them to Jerusalem reappeared and led them to a house in Bethlehem "where the young Child was" (Matthew 2:11). Notice that the appearance of the star brought "exceedingly great joy" to them (2:10).

The meaning of the three gifts has been a point of discussion from early Christianity. Gold has been interpreted as symbolizing worship of Jesus as king or a symbol of His virtue. Incense symbolized prayer, and myrrh symbolized suffering. Gregory the Great viewed the gold as a symbol of "wisdom, frankincense was the fragrant pursuit of holy speech, and myrrh the mortification of the flesh."[97]

As I have reflected on these gifts, it seems likely these gifts, which were expensive, provided the Holy Family with resources enabling the escape to Egypt, the time in Egypt, and the return trip to Nazareth in Galilee.

Titus 2:11; 3:4 – The Apostle Paul uses the Greek form of *epiphany*, and it is translated as "appeared" in both verses as he connects the manifestation of Christ to how we are to live in the world. The "appearance" of God in the world as "the Word made flesh" (John 1:14), as the Messiah of Israel (John 1:41), and as the Redeemer of the world (Matthew 1:21) is not myth or theological fantasy. Jesus has "appeared" to make a people from Jews and Gentiles who will live differently as witnesses to who He is and what He alone is able to do.

Titus 2:11 refers to Jesus "as the grace of God that brings salvation." Jesus is the ultimate manifestation of divine grace. His appearance "teaches" us how we should live. We live godly lives because we are "looking for the blessed hope and glorious appearing (there's that word *epiphany* again!) of our great God and Savior Jesus Christ."

The context of Titus 3:1-11 is how Christians behave before the "rulers and authorities," whether of civic government or governing the church. Titus 3:4, like 2:11, connects theological affirmations about Jesus with how we live. The "epiphany" of Jesus is the manifestation of "the kindness and love of God towards humanity." Martin Luther wrote that "kindness is the sweetness, not only goodness but kindness. A man is kind or sweet when he is friendly and well-disposed, easily approachable, not harsh but pleasant and joyful. He makes an effort to have people enjoy being around him. He is a brother to every man you can think of. This is a sweet manner."[98] Luther rightfully understood that this word applied to Jesus as the manifestation of the nature of divine love. The phrase "love of God towards humanity" is the translation of one Greek word meaning "love of humankind," φιλανθρωπία (*philanthropia*).

It is important to note that the epiphany of this kind of love is connected with "the washing of regeneration and renewing of the Holy Spirit" (3:6). The washing imagery is about water baptism and that this act constitutes a real change in the heart, mind, and actions of the believer.

From both Epiphany texts in Titus, it is clear that theological affirmations about the person of Jesus, His work, and how we live in the world are tied together, forming the presence of the "new creation" in the midst of the "old creation."

. . . TO SERMON

As you prepare to preach on the texts associated with Epiphany, keep in mind that if you start with Matthew 2 and the visit of the Magi, this is not another Christmas sermon. Though it closes the Twelve Days of Christmas, it introduces the church to the next phase of understanding Jesus and His message.

1. The primary theme of Matthew 2:1-12 as an Epiphany text is that the Gentile "wise men, kings, magi" come to worship Jesus. This is consistent with the Balaam oracles in Numbers 23 and 24. They represent

the wisdom and wealth of the world, ultimately bowing in submission to Jesus and His kingdom. Here are some passages that relate to this theme: Isaiah 11:10; 60:3 (an excellent verse related to the "star, light"), 5, 11, 16; 61:1. From these passages, you can develop preaching points related to our personal recognition of bowing before Jesus with our resources and with our minds and hearts.

2. If you choose to focus on the gifts of the Magi, you can further develop themes around the gold, frankincense, and myrrh. You should also develop how these gifts provided financial resources for the fleeing family and their return to Nazareth. The reality that God is our provider, Jehovah Jireh, based on Genesis 22:14, is a good place to preach on the "riches" we have in Jesus Christ. Several key texts in Paul's letters can be developed:

- 2 Corinthians 8:9 talks about Jesus and what He gave up in heaven.

- Ephesians 1:7 speaks of the riches of God's grace in forgiving our sins.

- Ephesians 1:18 refers to the riches of God's glory among the saints; that is, God's gifts among His people.

- Ephesians 2:4 – God is rich in mercy.

- Ephesians 2:7 speaks of the riches of His grace towards us.

- Ephesians 3:8 relates to preaching to the Gentiles the unsearchable riches of Christ.

- Ephesians 3:16 expresses the riches of His glory that strengthen us.

3. You can use Matthew 2:1-12 as a springboard for preaching about who Jesus is over the next weeks. Epiphany continues as a theme till Lent (usually mid-February). It's a great time to focus your preaching on Luke 2:41-52 and Jesus as a twelve-year-old; on Jesus' baptism accounts (Matthew 3:13-17; Mark 1:9-11; Luke 3:21, 22; John 1:29-36); Jesus' first miracle at Cana of Galilee (John 2:1-11); Jesus' temptations (Matthew 4:1-11; Mark 1:12, 13; Luke 4:1-13); Jesus' preaching in Nazareth, often called His inaugural address, Luke 4:16-30.

4. The Magi's recognition that Jesus is "the king of the Jews" is a good way to preach about the kingdom of God. The New Testament is clear

that this was one of the primary themes of Jesus' preaching (Mark 1:14, 15). The parables are about the kingdom of God (Matthew 13; Mark 4).

5. The Titus texts provide excellent ways to allow the Word of God to speak to how we live, talk, and act as God's people. You can avoid this kind of preaching of simple moralism by setting how we live within the context of the redemption given by Jesus and how we, as His followers, live as a "counter-culture" in our world. We are citizens of His kingdom before we are citizens of our nations. We belong to Him, and He has the final authority over our lives.

EPILOGUE

NOTES ON TEXT, PREPARATION, AND PREACHING

For the record, I'm not opposed to topical preaching. There are times when it's important to address certain topics from the standpoint of Scripture. What I think is important is that we are careful about "proof-texting" from the Bible to support points we wish to make related to the topic. The problem with "proof-texting" is that it is easy, perhaps convenient, to use a particular verse or even part of a verse, take it out of its biblical context, and force it to say something that, in reality, it does not intend to say.

This is why I am convinced the best preaching flows from the time spent with the biblical text allowing that text to speak from its historical, literary, and exegetical context. One might say, "Well, that means the text will only say one thing." Actually, that is not really true. Several factors mitigate against that kind of "end of the road" interpretation.

First, there is the ongoing work of the Holy Spirit in the life of the interpreter and the hearers. That work includes prayer, reflection, conversation with others, a growing range of experiences, and the recognition that the congregation is also being engaged by the Holy Spirit through their own devotional life and the dynamics of a particular worship service and its liturgy of prayers, music, etc.

Second, both the preacher and the congregation are different than they were some months or years earlier when they heard that text. We are more mature, or perhaps more desperate, than before. Often new people are in the seats when that text is preached again.

Besides using a lectionary structure of the biblical texts as an approach to Scripture, the preacher can determine to spend several weeks or even months preaching through a book of the Bible. Such expository preaching is easy on the preacher as his/her mind is already clear about the previous context, and usually has studied the entire book well enough to know where a particular text stands in relation to the whole.

The drawback to such preaching is that in much of the western world, far too many people simply do not attend the regular services consistently. A December 2021 study asked people in the US how often they attended church or synagogue. Twenty-two percent replied every week, and nine percent almost every week. That's essentially 30 percent of the church-attending population. Eleven percent replied about once a month, and twenty-five percent seldom.[99] In the post-Covid era of lockdowns, online services, and renewed in-person services, researchers and pastors are still trying to find how regular attendance will be determined.

It's the mixed bag of some people who almost always attend and some who come once or twice a month that makes expository preaching difficult on a particular book of the Bible or personality in the Bible. What does the preacher do to help that person who missed some of the sermons? Do we hope they took the time to watch it online? Perhaps what might help would be to provide a printed bulletin that included a couple of key paragraphs to help bring "up to speed" the person who usually misses a few Sundays each month! Something like, "In case you missed last Sunday;" then follow with a concise statement of the key points of the previous message.

Another option is for the pastor to keep the series to four or five messages and, once the series is completed, provide everyone with a printed document of the messages they can take home and hold in their hands for devotional reading. Or you might place a copy of the sermons on the church's website.

Another approach for long-term preaching preparation is for the pastor to put aside time to reflect prayerfully on what the Holy Spirit desires to speak to His church in the coming months or over the year. While a lectionary is a good resource, a pastor may be able to block out several weeks or even a month to simply read the Word, pray, and reflect on the messages that need to be given over the coming season.

Regardless of which path we take to discern the Lord's Word for a given time, several factors need to be considered.

Timing is essential. Starting to exegete, pray, and prepare on Saturday night for Sunday morning simply will not cut it. We might get by for a few weeks on the strength of personality or strong illustrations, but in the end, we are feeding God's sheep a weak diet. I suspect most of us are guilty of some of that, as the week was busy with pastoral care, funerals, denominational meetings, family commitments, etc. We come to Friday with the dreaded realization that Sunday is like a train racing down the tracks, and we don't have a clue what we are going to do! As Pentecostals, it's easy for us to say, "Well, we will let the Holy Spirit have His way this Sunday!" I'm afraid to think what the Holy Spirit thinks about our carelessness.

This is why it's imperative we carve out time in our schedules to be reading the Bible, praying, and preparing for sermons several weeks or even months in advance. This is where an awareness of the church calendar – Advent, Lent, Easter, Pentecost – comes in handy and where the use of a lectionary will lead us to texts found in the Old Testament, the Gospels, the New Testament Letters, and the Psalms.

To have time to prepare for the message is to treat the Word with the utmost respect. It gives time for prayer. We need to learn to "pray the text" as we come before the Lord. It is God's Word to His people, and as we hear that Word, we respond back to God by allowing the Holy Spirit to lead us in prayers related to the themes, words, and phrases of those texts. This kind of praying not only includes praying in our known language but includes praying in the Spirit. We pray in such a fashion over the Word of the text with confidence that the Holy Spirit is at work opening the eyes of our understanding (Ephesians 1:17).

Time gives us an opportunity to exegete and study the text. Each of us has our unique way of studying and using the resources with which we are most familiar. The key is to have the time to discern the meaning of the text clearly in its context.

A thought about the use of commentaries: If you do not understand the historical context of a biblical book or section, then a good commentary might provide that for you. There may be words or phrases that are unclear to you, and good commentaries will help. But let me caution you about running to a commentary to get a preaching idea you can use quickly. I personally think it's important to study the text as much as possible with the exegetical and language tools we can use before referring to commentaries. That does not mean you have to know Greek or Hebrew. Rather, compare the same text in various translations or paraphrases.

Good commentaries also help us avoid theological or interpretive errors of the text. If we think we have discovered a new teaching or doctrine, then more than likely, we have discovered an ancient heresy! If we are not certain that a particular point of the sermon is theologically correct, then don't use it. Find a more seasoned pastor or Bible school/seminary teacher with whom you can talk about these uncertainties. The congregation comes to hear the gospel and the message of the Bible, not our novel ideas.

Speaking of the novel, the new, it's tempting to get caught up in thinking we need to discover a "new teaching" to gain attention. While we clearly need to be engaging with the hearers, we are preachers who have the heavenly message of salvation revealed in the person of Jesus Christ in Holy Scripture. The Gospel is complete and does not need our additions.

In light of the current deficit of biblical knowledge in western society, our task is to present "the old, old story" in such a way that the hearer is confronted with the reality of its truth and hope.

Some preachers are very good at developing three-point outlines with memorable titles and alliteration. To be honest, I'm not very good at that, but I admire my colleagues who have that gift. I mention this because the heart of the sermon, the real thing(s) we believe the Holy Spirit is speaking for that occasion, should be the focus of the message.

But good communication usually needs a good introduction and conclusion. These elements cannot be crafted without our fully comprehending what the Holy Spirit is saying to us about the message of that text for that occasion. It's tempting to discover a great illustration and then build a sermon to fit it. The reality is that it takes time for the intent of the message to sink into our minds and spirits, and for the Holy Spirit to bring us the best way to lead into the text and the best way to lead out of the text.

You may not have noticed, but in the previous paragraph, I referenced "good communication." That was intentional. In most church traditions, "preaching" takes on a certain literary and oral style. Preaching is, indeed, very personal. It's an individual art. It's not uncommon for younger preachers to emulate preachers they have heard or who most influenced them. But the time comes when they discover their own voice. It's at that point that a deeper authenticity enters the unheard "dialogue" between the person behind the pulpit and the congregants. It's something we cannot "fake." It is rooted in discovering who we really are in Christ through prayer, Scripture, and being personally discipled by others. It means that we have moved past the need to be impressive, to be noticed, to be invited somewhere else as a "great preacher." That kind of authenticity is a maturing process and a willingness on our part to listen to the suggestions, and yes, criticisms, of those who love us most and who listen to us on a regular basis.

Somewhat related to "good communication" is the reality that most people listen differently than in previous generations. For instance, read the sermons of John Wesley, Charles Spurgeon, and others and ask if your congregation would listen to those sermons. Would you? I'm not suggesting that we should not read those sermons and learn from them. I'm suggesting that the average person in the western world does not have that attention span nor perhaps even the baseline knowledge to appreciate the impact of those sermons.

Sadly, we are accustomed to the "sound bites, entertainment, excitement" that is part of modern media communications. Have we succumbed to being "tweet" preachers?

Second, preaching is not a performance. Should we work to speak clearly, use proper grammar, and avoid distracting movements? Of course. But we need to remember that the focus is on Jesus, not us. That calls for a growing sense of humility. That comes from humbling ourselves to become constant disciples of Jesus. We are always like Mary, "sitting at His feet" (Luke 10:39). We should be willing to be criticized for hiding away in prayer and before the Word. It is easy for us to be busy in the public realm because it makes it appear we are "working." Our time in the closet of prayer and in the quiet rustling of printed or digital pages is where the real work is done. First, it is done in us as we are addressed by the Word. We become the audience the Holy Spirit is addressing. To be an audience of one before the One is to fall at His feet, crying out for mercy, receiving solace, and being empowered beyond our own strength of character, personality, knowledge, and wisdom.

Finally, I must confess that writing this epilogue may have been primarily an exercise to remind me of what I must be doing. I don't present myself as one who has been particularly successful in giving the time and study discussed in this chapter. In fact, I'm keenly aware of how much I have failed. But I'm also aware that "we have this treasure in earthen vessels, that the excellence of the power may be of God and not of us" (2 Corinthians 4:7). Our shortcomings are not excuses but are reminders of what more can be accomplished as we orient our time in Scripture and prayer.

I take solace in the Apostle Paul's confessions about his preaching in 1 Corinthians 2:1-5:

> And I, brethren, when I came to you, did not come with excellence of speech or of wisdom, declaring to you the testimony of God. I was with you in weakness, in fear, and in much trembling. And my speech and my preaching were not with persuasive words of human wisdom.

Yet for Paul, this self-awareness of lack did not keep him from preaching "Jesus Christ and Him crucified," and having confidence that his words, and the Word of the Cross, was "in demonstration of the Spirit and of power, that your faith should not be in the wisdom of men but in the power of God" (1 Corinthians 2:2, 4, 5).

For all of us who struggle with preaching, preparation, prayer, feelings of inadequacy, and with the curse of comparing ourselves to others, may we find that secret closet where the Holy Spirit will do His incomparable work of shaping us as disciples of Jesus through Scripture and prayer.[100]

ENDNOTES

1. There is a growing and significant amount of literature devoted to exploring Pentecostal hermeneutics. See Craig S. Keener, *Spirit Hermeneutics: Reading Scripture in Light of Pentecost* (Grand Rapids, MI: William B. Eerdmans Publishing Company, 2016); Gordon D. Fee, *Listening to the Spirit in the Text* (Grand Rapids, MI: William B. Eerdmans, 2000); Kenneth J. Archer, *A Pentecostal Hermeneutic: Spirit, Scripture and Community* (Cleveland, TN: CPT Press, 2009).

2. Advent usually begins in late November or early December.

3. The Twelve Days of Christmas are much more than a popular song!

4. Most readers of this book are part of what is called the Western Church tradition. That includes Roman Catholics, most Protestants and Pentecostals. The Western Church calendar is based on ancient church tradition and the Gregorian calendar. The Eastern Church is composed primarily of the Orthodox Churches from Greece, Russia, and Eastern Europe. The Eastern Church uses the Julian Calendar. Thus, their calendar will often be different from the Western Church calendar. There are Protestants and Pentecostals in the territories of the Eastern Church. Many of those churches maintain Western Church theologies but follow the Eastern Church calendar so as to fit into the cultural expressions of their nations.

5. The verb is advenire, "to come."

6. TULIP refers these elements of classical Calvinism and Reformed theology: Total depravity, Unconditional election, Limited Atonement, Irresistible grace, and Perseverance of the saints. For Arminian perspectives see Roger E. Olson, *Arminian Theology: Myths and Realities and Olson's Against Calvinism*.

7. I often use https://liturgical-calendar.com/en-emodeng/ACNA/2022-11-27 these days. It is the lectionary of the Anglican Church of North America (ACNA), a theologically conservative branch of the Church of England (Anglicans). I use this because the IPHC has theological roots in John Wesley and Methodism, and Wesley remained an Anglican minister his entire life. There are other lectionaries online and they follow a three-year cycle of going through the Bible.

8.   https://www.youtube.com/watch?v=u4ZoJKF_VuA. "The Golden Circle" starts with "Why?" then moves to "How?" and concludes with "What?"

9.   Thoughtful discussions of the ancient, non-Christian background of most religious holiday observances are found in *The Dance of Time: The Origins of the Calendar* by Michael Judge (New York, NY: Arcade Publishing, 2011). Judge shows how and why Christianity redefined numerous older sacred days and seasons. He describes how in the 16th and 17th centuries many Christians rejected this historic redefinition and abolished the practice of observing Christmas at all. Furthermore, he traces the development of the names of the months and days of the week after pagan festivals or Roman Emperors. Other than the efforts of atheistic and violently anti-Christian efforts in the French Revolution (1789-1799), I do not know any other efforts to totally remove all ancient and Christian identities from the calendar, including the names of months and days. Another resource related to the larger issues of calendars and time is David Ewing Duncan's *Calendar: Humanity's Epic Struggle to Determine a True and Accurate Year* (New York, NY: Avon Books, 1998).

10. Craig S. Keener, *The IVP Bible Background Commentary, Second Edition* (Downers Grove, IL: InterVarsity Press, 2014), 533.

11. An interesting example of this is expressed in a movement named Towards Jerusalem Council II (www.tjcii.org). The goal of this movement is to promote the view that Jewish followers of Yeshua (the Hebrew name of Jesus), should be able to practice their historic cultural Jewish life practices without forfeiting the clear New Testament revelation that we are justified by faith in Yeshua and not by works of the Torah (law).

12. Martin Luther, *Luther's Works: Lectures on Galatians*, Chapters 1-4 (St. Louis: Concordia Publishing House, 1963) 395, 396. Luther gave these lectures from July 2 through November 14. 1531. They were published in 1535.

13. Philip H. Pfatteicher, *Journey Into the Heart of God: Living the Liturgical Year* (New York: Oxford University Press, 2013) 9.

14. The quote is from Smith, *How (Not) To Be Secular: Reading Charles Taylor* (Grand Rapids, MI: William B. Eerdmans Publishing Co., 2014) 32. Taylor's *A Secular Age* (Belknap Press of Harvard University Press, Cambridge, MA, and London, England, 2007). Taylor's book is nearly 1000 pages, and we can all be grateful to Smith for condensing the main arguments into a more readable book.

15. The Enlightenment generally can be dated from the time of John Locke in the 1680s to the end of Napoleon I in 1815. This era marked a major change in how people view the world, themselves, and God.

16. For pastors in the United States, Advent often follows the American holiday of Thanksgiving. For pastors who usually centered late November preaching

around Thanksgiving, which is truly a good theme, there needs to be aware-ness of when Advent begins and reflection on how to connect these holidays together seamlessly for Sunday or other sermons. I encourage pastors to look at the liturgical calendar websites that were mentioned in the Introduction.

17. Referring to the Second Coming of Christ, see Matthew 24:3, 27, 37, 39, 1 Corinthians 15:23, 1 Thessalonians 2:19, 3:13, 4:15, 5:23, 2 Thessalonians 2:1, 8, 9, James 5:7, 8, 2 Peter 1:16, 3:4, 12, 1 John 2:28. The other four references are to the coming of colleagues of Paul or of Paul's coming himself to visit.

18. For discussions related to the concept of Parousia and its implications for eschatology see N.T Wright, *Jesus and the Victory of God* (Minneapolis, MN: Fortress Press, 1996) 341ff, and Wright's, *Surprised by Hope* (New York: HarperCollins Publishers, 2008) 128ff.

19. Pfatteicher, 28.

20. https://www.christianity.com/christian-life/christmas/what-is-advent.html is an excellent overview of the origins of Advent and contemporary practices.

21. Also see https://www.britannica.com/topic/Saturn-god. See also Pfatteicher, 33.

22. https://nationaltoday.com/orthodox-christmas-day/.

23. Judge, 171. See https://www.newworldencyclopedia.org/entry/Advent.

24. Judge, p. 177. See https://www.britannica.com/topic/Mithraism.

25. https://www.thegospelcoalition.org/blogs/kevin-deyoung/is-christmas-a-pagan-rip-off/.

26. Everyone in the Roman Empire was required to return to his birth city to pay this tax, and thus be counted.

27. It appears that the contemporary practices of hanging wreaths began in 1833 in Hamburg, Germany, by Johann Hinrich Wichern, who had founded a home for boys. Other practices predate Wichern, such as the rose as a popular Christian symbol based on Isaiah 35:1, 2 and associated with the Virgin Mary (probably 13th century). In the 15th century, the hymn, "Lo, How a Rose E'er Blooming," began to be sung, symbolizing Christ as the rose. See Pfatteicher, pp. 68, 69.

28. Some traditions have three purple candles for the first three Sunday, then a pink candle, the Joy Candle, for the fourth Sunday, with the larger white candle, the Christ candle, in the center. See https://www.youtube.com/watch?v=XILTfuN3ahM for an example. In most churches, taller candles should be used rather than the smaller ones in this video. There are numerous Advent video demonstrations on YouTube for home devotional use or for the church service.

29. Barry G. Webb, *The Message of Isaiah* (Downers Grove, IL: IVP Academic, 1996). I'm using Webb's dates in these studies in Isaiah.

30. Mark Rutland, *Of Kings and Prophets* (Lake Mary, FL: Charisma House, 2021). Though Rutland does not specifically discuss Isaiah, this is nonetheless a good study with contemporary application of the dynamics of prophets and civic leaders.

31. Walter Brueggemann, *Isaiah 40-66* (Louisville, KY: Westminster John Knox Press, 1998), 3. The division of Isaiah into three sections has been characteristic of critical scholarship since the landmark study of Bernhard Duhm in 1883 (Barry Webb, p. 34).

32. "The Holy One of Israel" is an important phrase in this prophecy. It is used 12 times in 1-39 and 13 times in 40-66.

33. My view does not discount the possibility that Isaiah had a "school of prophetic disciples" (Isaiah 8:16) who outlived him and helped to edit the entire book in its present form. That is not a denial of the inspiration or authority of the entire book. Just as the Holy Spirit anointed Isaiah, He easily could have anointed those who were faithful to Isaiah's message and understanding. For more on these issues see Webb, pp. 33-37, and *New Bible Commentary*, edited by D.A. Carson, R.T. France, J.A. Motyer, and G.J. Wenham (Downers Grove, IL: Inter-Varsity Press, 1994) pp. 630-632. For preaching purposes, there is little reason to discuss these authorship questions in any detail in a sermon. It is appropriate in discussing passages in Isaiah 40-66 to refer to their message as dealing with the Jews in exile and post-exile, and it is appropriate to speak of the Holy Spirit giving Isaiah a clear vision of events that lay in the future as far as he was concerned when he received them.

34. Brueggemann, p. 8.

35. Brueggemann, p. 11. Italics used in the source.

36. *Dead Sea Scrolls, The Rule of the Community*, cited by G.K. Beale and D.A. Carson, editors, *Commentary on the New Testament Use of the Old Testament* (Grand Rapids, MI: Baker Academic, 2007) 12, 13.

37. Ahaz reigned from 735-715 B.C.

38. In understanding much of the Old Testament, it is imperative that the student of the Bible comprehend the history of Israel's united and divided monarchy. The first king Saul was from the tribe of Benjamin and had he been faithful to God's call, his lineage may have reigned longer. The second king, David from Bethlehem, united the 12 tribes under his capital at Jerusalem (2 Samuel 2 for David's reign over Judah; 2 Samuel 5 for David's reign over the 12 tribes). The "United Monarchy" continued through the reign of Solomon. However, Solomon's son, Rehoboam, was an unwise ruler and his oppressive policies led to a revolt by Jeroboam who led ten of the northern tribes in a successful rebellion

which led to the "Divided Monarchy." The consequences of this divisive Israelite civil war are the content of 1 Kings 12 - 2 Kings 17; 2 Chronicles 10 (which focuses on the history of the southern kingdom of Judah and Benjamin), and the prophets Elijah, Elisha, Amos, Hosea, Micah, Isaiah among others. The "kings of Israel" are considered apostate and rebellious against the Lord as they advocated the worship of idols and were supportive of abusive and unjust policies. To "walk in the way of the kings of Israel" was never a compliment.

39. While not part of the specific historical situation in Isaiah 7, the prophet Jonah prophesied in the mid-700s B.C. The book of Jonah gives the account of his reluctant ministry to Nineveh, the capital of Assyria. It shows that God was work in this growing empire decades before Assyria became the dominant threat against Palestine. While Nineveh repented in response to the word of judgment, the spirit of conversion, genuine long lasting change, did not follow.

40. How Isaiah was frustrated by the foolishness of Ahaz is seen in Isaiah 7:13. It is important to keep in mind that Ahaz was probably a teenager when his grandfather, Uzziah, died. Ahaz would have known of his grandfather's leprosy and why he was judged by God. This adds to the rebellious and ungodly nature of Ahaz and the total moral and spiritual corruption of this Judean leader.

41. Rezin reigned in Syria from 740-732 and Pekah in Israel from 737-732. Barry Webb dates the crisis of Isaiah 7 at the year 734 (The Message of Isaiah, 61).

42. "Ephraim" was a synonym for the 10 northern tribes called Israel.

43. Commentators differ on the identity of the 'son of Tabel.' In some sources the name is spelled "Tabeel." He may have been from the Northern Kingdom of Israel or from Syria. Regardless, the plan was to forcibly remove Ahaz and replace him with this person.

44. Our English word amen is an adverb form of the Hebrew verb aman. In a sense, to believe God's Word is to amen God; that is, to say that I agree with God's Word. For God to amen us is His act of establishing what He has promised to us in His Word.

45. Walter Brueggemann, Isaiah 1-39 (Louisville, KY: Westminster John Knox Press, 1998) 70.

46. Often Immanuel is spelled in English as Emmanuel. I will use the Immanuel spelling as it is the spelling used in the New King James Version. The meaning is exactly the same.

47. *Luther's Works, Volume 16, Lectures on Isaiah, Chapters 1-39* edited by Jaroslav Pelikan and Hilton C. Oswald (St. Louis, MO: Concordia Publishing House, 1969) 84.

48. *Wesley's Notes on the Bible*, edited by G. Roger Schoenhals (Grand Rapids, MI: Francis Asbury Press, 1987) 324.

49. Rev. Noel Brooks, "The Incarnation and Virgin Birth of Christ," The Pentecostal Holiness Advocate, February 14, 1970, page 23.

50. It's interesting that very little is said about Isaiah's wife, other than she was a prophetess. She is not identified by name but by her relation to Isaiah and what appears to have been a spiritual gift.

51. Uriah is clearly identified as a "cohen," a priest. Zechariah is not the prophet whose written prophecy is found in the Old Testament. The identity of the Zechariah in Isaiah 8 is uncertain. Among the options which correspond to the time in which Isaiah lived are a) 2 Chronicles 26:5, he is the Zechariah who "had understanding in the visions of God"; that is, a court prophet who influenced Uzziah and therefore could have been a prophetic mentor to Isaiah; b) he may have been the father-in-law of King Ahaz making him the maternal grandfather of King Hezekiah (2 Kings 18:1, 2; 2 Chronicles 29:1). It's possible he was both.

52. Notice the repetition of the names of the Syrian and Northern Kingdom rulers.

53. Shiloah was a fountain southeast of Jerusalem.

54. 1 Samuel 15:22-26; 28:3-25; note that Saul's disobedience in 1 Samuel 15 is described "as the sin of witchcraft"": Saul's actions in 1 Samuel 28 relate to his visit to the medium at En Dor.

55. The Assyrian ruler Tiglath-pileser III annexed these territories from Israel in 733 (2 Kings 15:29). The two tribes were on a major route northwest and west of the Sea of Galilee and provided the best entrance into the remainder of the land of Israel.

56. A good read about Jesus' saying in Matthew 11 is Gentle and Lowly: *The Heart of Christ for Sinners and Sufferers* by Dane Orlund (Wheaton, IL: Crossway, 2020).

57. Walter Brueggemann, *Names for the Messiah: An Advent Study* (Louisville, KY: Westminster John Knox Press, 2016) pp. 1-3. Brevard Childs, *Isaiah: A Commentary* (Louisville, KY: Westminster John Knox Press), Kindle edition location 2275.

58. https://petersonhist127.weebly.com/the-vacant-chair.html.

59. Brevard S. Childs, *Isaiah: A Commentary* (Louisville, KY: Westminster John Knox Press, 2001). Kindle location 2593. The "Syro" refers to Syria (Damascus) and Ephraim refers to the dominant tribe of the Northern Kingdom.

60. Childs, Kindle location 2629.

61. Some commentators take Hezekiah to be the "Rod from the stem of Jesse;" (Isaiah 11:1), a reference to a godly king taking the place of the ungodly Ahaz. Most commentators acknowledge the difficulty of precise dating in Isaiah's

oracles except where the prophet specifically does so. This difficulty is evident in Isaiah 10, 11 in attempting to give a precise date. Isaiah does not name the Judean king, though the flow of the passages from Isaiah 7-11 seem to give credence to the time of Ahaz.

62. See Isaiah 10:20-26 for the combination of "remnant" and the victory at Midian.

63. Barry G. Webb, *The Message of Isaiah* (Downers Grove, IL: IVP Academic, 1996), 75.

64. Hebrew for banner is *nes* (נס).

65. The issue of identity is particularly important in a time when identity in the West is politicized in race, gender, and sexual acts. A good introduction to this is Carl R. Trueman's *Strange New World: How Thinkers and Activists Redefined Identity and Sparked the Sexual Revolution* (Wheaton, Ill: Crossway, 2022).

66. Michael Judge, *The Dance of Time, The Origins of the Calendar: A Miscellany of History and Myth, Religion and Astronomy, Festivals and Feast Days* (New York: Arcade Publishing, 2004) 177. The Mithras cult was combined with an older Roman December festival named Saturnalia which Judge described as "a city-wide orgy" (176).

67. The celebration of Christmas on December 25 was seriously challenged in England in the 1640s when Oliver Cromwell established the British Commonwealth. With his strong Protestant leanings, Cromwell rejected many Christian practices that had evolved over previous centuries. This included holidays such as Christmas and influenced many American colonists in New England who also rejected Christmas festivities." (Judge, pp. 180, 181).

68. An excellent resource for tracking OT texts and their use in the New Testament is Gleason L. Archer & G.C. Chirichigno, *Old Testament Quotations in the New Testament: A Complete Survey* (Chicago: Moody Press, 1983) 94-98.

69. Raymond E. Brown, *The Birth of the Messiah: A Commentary on the Infancy Narratives in Matthew and Luke* (Garden City, NY: Image Books, a Division of Doubleday & Company, Inc., 1979).

70. Brown, pp. 71-74.

71. Alfred Edersheim, *The Life and Times of Jesus the Messiah* (Grand Rapids, MI: William B. Eerdmans Publishing Co., 1986 reprint edition), 148-150. Also see William Hendriksen, *Exposition of the Gospel According to Matthew* (Grand Rapids, MI: Baker Book House, 1973) 130.

72. Also, it is not coincidental that the account of the first woman named in the Matthean genealogy, Tamar, occurs in Genesis 38 as part of the Joseph Genesis narrative.

73. This does not imply any "seduction" or "immorality" on Mary's part in this unique situation. Rather, in the natural eyes of Joseph and the community she would be viewed as immoral.

74. The "Western" churches are Roman Catholic and most Protestant. "Eastern" churches are the various Orthodox churches (Greek, Russian, etc.). If you are wondering about the visit of the Magi in Matthew 2, that text will be described in the next chapter as that is one of the primary texts for Epiphany.

75. John Bright remarked that the 582 deportation was probably a continuation of the deportation that occurred five years earlier with Jerusalem's destruction. A History of Israel (Philadelphia, PA: The Westminster Press, 1972, 331). Some commentators place the first deportation in the late 600s.

76. A comment by Matthew in 2:1 that has interesting overtones to the reference of "the land of the East" in Genesis 29:1. It is likely the Magi came from Babylon and would have known Jewish writings from the Jews who remained following the end of the Babylonian exile.

77. *Dictionary of Jesus and the Gospels*, edited by Joel B. Green, Jeannine K. Brown, & Nicholas Perrin (Downers Grove, IL: IVP Academic, 2013) 380-381.

78. It is generally recognized that Jesus was born about 4-6 B.C., and Herod's death is usually placed at 4 B.C. This dating system began in 525 A.D. by Dionysius Exiguus and by the 800s A.D. was popularly used. He was a monk in Rome and later it was determined his division between B.C. and A.D. was off by less than a decade.

79. Raymond Brown discussed the details of this Matthew 2:23 on pages 207-213. On pages 223, 224 he gave his personal view that Matthew tied the place name where Jesus grew up, Nazareth, because it was similar in sound to the Hebrew word Branch (*neser*), and because Jesus was a Nazirite (*Nazir*), "the Holy One, dedicated to God's service since birth. It is this last derivation that Matthew has in mind when he says, 'that what was spoken by the prophets might be fulfilled,'" (223). In Brown's interpretation, Matthew has in mind Isaiah 4:3 and Judges 16:17. He shows the connections between the Hebrew Masoretic text and the LXX, both of which would have been familiar to Matthew.

80. https://blog.israelbiblicalstudies.com/jewish-studies/jerusalem-synagogue-freedmen-prof-peter-shirokov-eteacherbiblical/.

81. https://www.newadvent.org/cathen/11604a.htm.

82. https://www.supremecourt.gov/opinions/21pdf/19-1392_6j37.pdf. This US Supreme Court decision was announced on June 24, 2022.

83. https://earlychurchhistory.org/martyrs/christian-martyrs-now/.

84. https://www.persecution.com/.

85. At Epiphany the Western Church emphasizes the visit of the Magi to Jesus while the Eastern Church (Orthodox Christians) emphasizes Jesus' baptism and His first miracle at Cana of Galilee. IPHC missionary Russell Board and Beacham wrote a series of essays titled *Christmas: Before and After*, that is available at https://www.amazon.com/Christmas-Before-After-Doug-Beacham-ebook/dp/B00A7XJ3LC/

86. Act 2, Scene 5. Shakespeare wrote this play in either 1601 or 1602 as entertainment at the close of the Christmas season in England. A romantic comedy, the lines were uttered by Malvolio, steward to the Countess Olivia.

87. Revelation 2:1-7; John 4:23, 24.

88. My hope regarding this emphasis on preaching the Bible themes is not based on a narrow view of preaching or on a rejection of the culture. Rather, my emphasis is on the larger hermeneutical issue of "narrative." What narrative, or storyline, will we allow to be the central theme for God's sheep for whom we are accountable? Do we allow the narrative of our societies to be the focus on our lives, or do we allow the Word of God and the narrative of divine revelation to be the determining storyline of our lives? Obviously in preaching on these dates one can naturally refer to the events and occasions that are part of our secular story. But the focus needs to remain on the biblical texts and what it reveals about God's intentions for us.

89. Luke's account condensed the time the Holy Family was in Bethlehem, not recording what Matthew 2 included. A simple reading of Luke 2 without reference to Matthew 2 fails to acknowledge the actual time the family was in Bethlehem and then in Egypt. In *The Birth of the Messiah: A Commentary on the Infancy Narratives in Matthew and Luke*, Raymond Brown explains the differences between Matthew and Luke's timelines as occurring because the two writers did not know one another (pp. 497-499). This is a reasonable conjecture as Matthew, who was a disciple of Jesus and knew Mary, had distinct reasons for including, and excluding, various parts of the birth of Jesus. On the other hand, Luke, who apparently was a Gentile, included parts of the birth narrative that Matthew certainly knew but chose not to focus upon.

90. The 'Bet' is house and "lehem' is bread.

91. https://www.bethlehem-city.org/en/history-of-bethlehem#:~:text=Two%20Roman%20ladies%20of%20noble,some%20interruption%2C%20to%20this%20day.

92. Other villages in Israel were named Bethlehem. Given the agricultural predominance of the economy, it should be expected that towns named "house of bread," would be somewhat common. In Scripture the Bethlehem of David and Jesus is usually associated with another place name such as Judah (Judges

17:7, 9, 9, 19:1, 2, Ruth 1,1) or Ephrathah (Micah 5:2). In light of this, some commentators do not include the Israelite judge Ibzan as being from the Judean Bethlehem (Judges 12:8-10).

93. Brown, op. cit., pp. 166-183. My personal view is that they likely came from Babylon as many Jews remained in Babylon following the close of the exile (ca. 538 B.C.). The Babylonian Talmud dates from the Christian era though it may reflect rabbinic debates and views held among Jews in Babylon following the exile and at the time of Christ.

94. Brown, pp.170-174. Many of the early church fathers did not believe this was an actual celestial star but rather a specific light given by the Holy Spirit to guide the Magi to the home of the Christ Child.

95. Though 2:8 is on the lips of Herod the Great, its usage from him not only reveals his duplicity but also a subtle recognition that this Child is not to be ignored by the court.

96. Think of the popular Christmas carol, "We Three Kings."

97. *Ancient Christian Commentary on Scripture, New Testament IA*, Matthew 1-13, edited by Manlio Simonetti, General Editor Thomas C. Oden (Downers Grove, IL: InterVarsity Press, 2001) pp. 25, 28. The quoted section is from Simonetti's overview on page 25.

98. *Martin Luther, Luther's Works, Lectures on Titus, Philemon, and Hebrews*, Volume 29, Jaroslav Pelikan, Editor (St. Louis, MO: Concordia Publishing House, 1968), 78.

99. https://www.statista.com/statistics/245491/church-attendance-of-americans/. You may also find this article by Carey Nieuwhof useful: https://careynieuwhof.com/5-smarter-ways-to-embrace-infrequent-church-attenders/.

100. James D. Leggett, editor. *Preaching to Connect: An Anthology of Sermons and Practical Insights* (Franklin Springs, GA: LifeSprings Resources, 2005). This is a collection of 18 sermons and preaching essays by ministers in the International Pentecostal Holiness Church.

Dr. A.D. (Doug) Beacham has been General Superintendent of the International Pentecostal Holiness Church since 2012. Previously he served as Executive Director of both IPHC World Missions Ministries and IPHC Discipleship Ministries, Georgia Conference Superintendent, pastor of the Franklin Springs Pentecostal Holiness Church, and instructor at Emmanuel College. From 1977-2001 he served as a chaplain in the United States Army Reserves. He represents the IPHC on numerous interdenominational boards and committees, including the National Association of Evangelicals, Pentecostal and Charismatic Churches of North America, and the Pentecostal World Fellowship.

He and his wife Susan Reed Beacham have been married over fifty years. Their daughter Beth is an attorney in Alexandria, Virginia, and their son A.D. Beacham, III is a physician in Oklahoma City. They have two granddaughters, Caroline and Lib, who live in Oklahoma City.

Beacham is a graduate of Emmanuel College, the University of Georgia, and Union Theological Seminary (now Union Presbyterian Seminary) in Richmond, Virginia.

Acknowledgements

Several people have read this manuscript and offered insights and corrections that have been included. A special thanks to Mrs. Shirley Spencer, former editor of IPHC literature for her thorough edit of the manuscript. Dr. Ryan Jackson and Dr. Kenneth Young reviewed my use of Greek and Hebrew. Dr. Cheryl Bridges-Johns, Dr. Terry Tramel, and Rev. Chris Maxwell read the manuscript and offered helpful insights. I am grateful for the encouragement and patience of publisher Steve Spillman in seeing this book to completion. For any errors that remain, or questionable interpretations, those remain my responsibility.

www.ingramcontent.com/pod-product-compliance
Lightning Source LLC
LaVergne TN
LVHW051811080426
835513LV00017B/1908